HOW TO MOVE HOUSE SUCCESSFULLY

ANNE CHARLISH is best known as a medical writer who specializes in making complex medical topics accessible to the general reader. Her previous books include *How to Cure Your Ulcer* (Sheldon Press 1988) and *A Woman's Guide to Birth-tech: Tests and Technology in Pregnancy and Birth* (Christopher Helm 1989). Anne Charlish is also the author of *Home Security* and *First Aid and Home Safety* (both Ward Lock 1988). She also writes consumer and fashion features for women's magazines such as *Homes & Gardens*.

For a complete list of titles in the **Overcoming Common Problems** Series write to:

Sheldon Press,
SPCK, Marylebone Road, London NW1 4DU

Overcoming Common Problems

HOW TO MOVE HOUSE SUCCESSFULLY

Anne Charlish

SHELDON PRESS
LONDON

First published in Great Britain 1989
Sheldon Press, SPCK, Marylebone Road, London NW1 4DU

© Anne Charlish 1989

British Library Cataloguing in Publication Data
  Charlish, Anne
    How to move house successfully.
    1. Great Britain. Residences. Removal – Practical information
    I. Title   II.Series
    648'.9'0941

    ISBN 0–85969–589–1

      Typeset by Deltatype Ltd, Ellesmere Port, Cheshire
Printed in Great Britain by Courier International Ltd, Tiptree, Essex

Contents

Note

Tax rates mentioned in the book refer to those for 1989–90 as announced by the Chancellor of the Exchequer in March 1988. If you are quoted any figures involving either tax or tax relief, be sure to check that the assumed tax rate accords with your own. Tax rates and tax relief are subject to change with each Government Budget, as announced by the Chancellor, in March of each year. Your tax office or your accountant will give you this information.

Author's note

I would like to thank Laurence Mann for his last-minute intervention in a number of important transactions and his unfailing courtesy and wit.

Introduction

Moving house can often seem something of a nightmare. Even if we are lucky enough not to have our own horror stories to tell, most of us have heard enough of other people's to dread moving. Most of the real disasters, though, can be averted – with some basic skills and a bit of advance planning. Turning up at your new home, with everything on board the removals van, to find that it is still occupied and they won't let you in is an example of something that couldn't happen with good planning and good liaison, as this book is intended to show.

'Gazumping' – in which the vendor of a property withdraws acceptance of one offer in favour of another, higher, one – is something that's difficult to prevent but there are things that buyers in England and Wales can do to avoid it, as you'll see in Chapter 2. Fortunately, if you are buying in Scotland, it can't happen to you. The Scottish legal process for buying a new home is rather different than the system that currently exists in England and Wales. Buyers in Scotland still have to find their way through a maze of practical details, however, to make sure of a smooth move, just as buyers elsewhere do. When I bought and sold a house for the first time, I was astonished at the amount of paperwork involved, and astonished, particularly, at the number of different things to be understood.

The confusing and sometimes alarming business of moving is one in which it helps to have some mathematical ability (for it is, indeed, a business) and one in which you need to understand three new languages – that of estate agents, that of surveyors and that of solicitors. Many professionals make the flattering mistake from time to time of assuming that we know as much as they do: for this reason, they sometimes fail to explain things fully, or, when they do, they fall back on mystifying jargon. Not all of us understand, for example, what is meant by 'rainwater goods', 'the payments can be rolled over', 'contract race' and 'reduced deposit monies passing up the chain'.

The first golden rule is to keep a budget, and to ask, each time you are quoted a figure, 'Is that an estimate or a firm quotation?', and 'Does that attract VAT?'. If it does, remember to add 15 per cent, so that £100 instantly becomes £115 and £1000 turns into £1150. You can see how things might mount up. It's easy to see why a budget may need continual revision or, in some cases, simply collapse. Chapter 1 describes all the expected costs of moving, as well as some of the unexpected. Many first-time buyers may find it hard to believe, for example, that they will have to find well over £100, perhaps £150, if they wish to have a telephone installed in a newly converted flat where there is no existing line. Keeping an eye on the budget is a theme that runs right through this book.

Estate agents are positive souls, and therefore present anything they'd like to sell in the most glowing terms possible: they have their own language, as you will see in Chapter 2. Surveyors, however, are of a gloomier disposition: they, too, have their own language, as you will discover in Chapter 3. Whereas an agent may typically describe a property as 'stunning', a surveyor would characteristically describe the same place as 'acceptable'. Conversely, if an agent admits a need for 'modernization', a surveyor will paint the blackest picture imaginable and do everything possible in his lengthy report to put you off it. This is not to diminish the importance of such reports, however. No one should consider investing in property without first obtaining a surveyor's full report – which is not the same as a valuation.

Solicitors, too, have their own language, and I hope that Chapters 3 and 4 will help you to unravel the mysteries of the contract and the legal questions that typically beset buyers in England and Wales. Things are different in Scotland. If you are buying in Scotland, and your offer has been accepted, you may skip right over Chapter 4 and into Chapter 5, past exchange of contracts, to the practical issues.

Good planning and anticipation are the key to a smooth move. I hope that the many points of detail covered in Chapters 5, 6 and 7 will help take the horror out of moving in whatever part of the country you have chosen to buy your new home.

INTRODUCTION

When we are in the throes of moving, with all its chaos and uncertainty, many of us declare, 'Never, ever again'. And yet the challenge and excitement of finding a new home and settling into it, especially for the first-time buyer, are hard to resist. I hope that this book relieves you of the worries and helps you to enjoy the challenge and the excitement of your next move to the full.

Anne Charlish
Sussex, 1989

1

How much can I spend?

Moving house is not unlike running a small business for several months. There may be prolonged negotiations in selling your existing property, if you have one; and buying a new property with its complex legal and financial aspects can prove daunting. Although moving house can often be a profoundly emotional event, it is best regarded as a business venture. Moving is well known to be a most stressful event for most of us, third only after bereavement and divorce. The stress of moving house is probably caused partly by prolonged uncertainty about your home, followed by disorientation when you do eventually move, combined with money worries.

Buying a home in England and Wales is particularly stressful in that nothing is certain until you have exchanged contracts with the vendor of the property (see Chapter 3). In Scotland, however, the whole process is less fraught: once your offer is accepted, you are committed to the purchase – you can't make an offer subject to survey and contract as in England and Wales. If you propose to buy a home in Scotland, you have to arrange for the lender's valuation and your own survey to be carried out *before* you make your offer.

Sorting out the money, and budgeting for all the different costs associated with moving, is something that can be done in a businesslike fashion. You can to some extent reduce the stress of moving by appreciating at the outset exactly what you are letting yourself in for. It's tempting, of course, not to think about it but this can lead later in the negotiations, or after you have moved, to a feeling that you are about to be submerged in a tidal wave of debt.

The first step is to work out how much you have available to spend on your new home. Putting it simply, this is the amount of money you have, added to the cash realized from selling your existing property after paying off the mortgage, minus the costs of moving, added to the new mortgage you can raise. To illustrate this, apply your own figures to the sum below:

£	
2,000	in bank deposit account
+ 85,000	sale of your existing property
87,000	
− 71,000	outstanding mortgage to be repaid to building society or bank
16,000	
− 7,000	cost of moving
9,000	
+ 100,000	amount of new mortgage that building society or bank will allow
109,000	total available for purchase

These figures show that this particular house-hunter can look at properties priced at over £100,000 and up to £110,000 (assuming that it will be possible to negotiate £1000 off the asking price of £110,000). It would not be realistic to look at properties of £115,000 or more, for example, because even if you succeeded in negotiating £2000 off the price, you would still have to find the considerable sum of £4000.

What it costs to move

The biggest variable item in calculating how much you have to spend is the cost of moving. You should be able to establish quite soon how much you can realistically hope to realize on any existing property, and you can also find out from a building society or bank how much they are prepared to lend you to buy your new home, on the basis of your income and that of your partner.

The cost of moving varies, partly because it comprises a large number of different costs and partly because it will depend on your attitude to settling into a new home. For example, is it essential for you to have a telephone? Transferring an existing one to your name or installing a new one can cost over £100. Do you consider it essential to have carpets and curtains right from the start? Using the fixed costs checklist below and the additional costs checklist later in this chapter, you can work out a realistic budget; provided that you consider only properties within your price limit, you stand a better chance of avoiding a tidal wave of debt in the future.

Fixed costs

Although each will vary according to the price of the property you are buying, the following expenditures must be allowed for in your budget:

1 A deposit to be paid to the estate agent once you have found a property that you like. This deposit can vary, according to the price of the property, from £100 to £500 or more. It is not, either in fact or in law, a 'fixed cost': it is not legally binding either on you as the buyer or on the vendor, and you may decline to pay it. However, I have included it as a fixed cost simply because many estate agents regard the payment of such a deposit as an 'expression of good faith' and as a sign that you are committed to going ahead with the purchase of the property. If another potential buyer makes an offer for the property at about the same time as you, your deposit may ensure that you are regarded as a serious buyer by the estate agent and are recommended by him to the vendor.

Be sure to keep track of any deposit paid. Obtain a signed and dated receipt for it at the time and inform your solicitor that a deposit has been paid. If your solicitor is overseeing all financial matters for you, it is a simple matter for the solicitor to deduct any deposit paid to the agent from the main deposit payable on exchange of contracts. Bear in mind that if the transaction does not proceed to exchange of contracts, you may ask for your deposit to be returned.

2 You will at some point in the negotiation before exchange of contracts have to find a percentage of the purchase price of your new property – to be paid as a deposit. The percentage is normally 10 per cent but this can be negotiated; the minimum deposit that is acceptable is 5 per cent. Strictly speaking, if you do negotiate, and you are buying and selling at the same time, you should give and receive the same percentages on both deals. In other words, you should not arrange to pay a reduced deposit on your purchase and at the same time refuse to allow your own buyer to pay a similarly reduced deposit. Equally – again, strictly speaking – if your buyer pays the full 10 per cent deposit, you should pay the full 10 per cent deposit. In practice, however, particularly in long chains of buyers and sellers, this does not always happen: the deposit monies tend to represent a smaller and smaller percentage as they travel up the chain. Because people tend to buy a more expensive property than the one they are selling, the amount of money involved is still considerable even though it may not represent a full 10 per cent deposit.

If you are buying at £100,000, therefore, you may need to find £10,000. This problem is partly overcome if you already own a property, as you will receive 10 per cent of your selling price – £8500 if your property sells for £85,000, for example – and you will therefore only have to find the difference, £1500 in this example. It is most important to talk to your solicitor about the 'deposit monies' well before exchange of contracts, particularly if you are involved in a chain of buyers and sellers.

3 The cost of the lender's valuation, the lender's legal fees, and their arrangement fee, which, together, will probably amount to more than £250 in 1989. The lender is the building society or bank, which will put a value on the property of your choice before agreeing to lend you the money to buy it to make sure that it is worth the asking price. This valuation is often referred to as a survey, which it is not. It should be regarded *only* as a valuation and cannot be relied upon as a surveyor's report on the property. The lender will incur legal fees in granting you a mortgage and will pass these on to you. Ask your building society or bank for a *quotation* (not an estimate) of the costs for valuation, their legal fees, their arrangement fee (for arranging the loan) and any other fee that they normally charge. Ask which of these charges attract VAT and allow for that at the rate of 15 per cent.

4 The cost of your own survey of the property, which may amount to several hundred pounds. Do select a surveyor as early as you can, find out what he will charge, adding VAT at the rate of 15 per cent. Surveyor's reports are discussed in more detail later in this chapter and in Chapter 3. For a full structural survey of a four-bedroom house in 1989, for example, one must think in terms of £500, and perhaps £300 for a two-bedroom flat.

5 Costs determined by the lender's valuation (point 3 above). These are works considered necessary by the lender as a condition of their agreement to grant you a mortgage on a particular property. These building works, which can include, for example, remedying problems with dry rot, damp rot, woodworm, defective gutters or a leaking roof, are also discussed at greater length in this chapter. Allow for VAT at 15 per cent on top of any quotation or estimate.

6 The fee for a relocation agent's services, usually charged at 1–1½ per cent of your purchase price, plus VAT at 15 per cent. It is usually only the wealthy who commission relocation agents to do their house-hunting and house-buying for them. These agents' services are discussed in more detail later in this chapter and in Chapter 2.

7 The fee to be paid to the estate agent who sells your existing property, unless you elect to market and sell your home yourself. The estate agent's fee can vary from £500 to £6000 or more, depending on the selling price of the property and the basis on which you retain the agent, and you must budget for VAT to be added at 15 per cent. These variables are discussed in detail on page 30.

8 Your legal fees. You can establish what these are to be, even before you start house-hunting, by finding a solicitor, telling him/her the price ranges of your sale and your purchase, asking for a quotation (not an estimate) and adding VAT at 15 per cent. The legal fees for conveyancing are unlikely to be under £300 plus VAT for the purchase of a property and this figure can be doubled if you are also selling a property. The combined fees can amount to over £1000, depending on the value of the properties and the type of solicitor you choose. Choosing a solicitor is discussed in detail later in this chapter.

9 Stamp duty. This is a fee levied by the Government of 1 per cent on properties bought at more than £30,000. If you are buying at £85,000, therefore, you will have to budget for stamp duty of £850. If you are buying at £200,000, you will have to allow for £2000. Your solicitor will be able to confirm the current stamp duty percentage and the threshold at which it is applied.

10 Land Registry fee. Again, this is calculated on a sliding scale, details of which you can obtain from your solicitor or direct from the Land Registry (tel: 01-405 3488). Examples of current charges are £50 on a £40,000 purchase price, £80 on £60,000, £160 on £100,000, £180 on £150,000, £200 on £200,000, and £225 on £250,000.

11 The cost of utilities (water, gas, electricity and telephone). There may be unavoidable charges for the transfer of these services from one houseowner to another or for their installation. Bear in mind that some building societies and banks will not lend money on a property unless they are installed. Costs vary, so do check with each board or company – and don't forget about VAT at 15 per cent.

12 The cost of removal. You may be able to move yourself by hiring a van and talking friends into helping you, particularly if you are a first-time buyer. Get several companies to visit your home, if you intend to be moved professionally, and ask for written quotations. Moving the contents of a four-bedroomed family house can easily make a hole in £1000 and will also attract VAT at 15 per cent.

13 The moving budget must also incude a realistic apprai-sal of outgoings once you have moved. These include, principally: the mortgage repayments each month, the rates bill, service charges (often applied to flats), (all of which are discussed in more detail later in this chapter); as well as building insurance on your new purchase (which is made practically obligatory by the building society or bank and which has to come into effect from the time of exchange of contracts), contents insurance (a wise precaution), and bills for water, gas, electricity and telephone, as well as a sum for your normal personal expenditure.

Yes, it is indeed horrifying . . . and once you have worked your way through points 1–13 above (perhaps leaving out points 5, 6 and 13 – building works, relocation agent and regular monthly outgoings), it is easy to see that moving house can very easily cost £7000 and may soar to £20,000–£30,000 if you are buying in the £200,000–£250,000 price range. It is little wonder that doctors recognize that moving house is a highly stressful activity, even though just a few of us actually thrive on it!

Do you need to move?

Now that you have bought a book on the subject of coping successfully with moving house, you may find it difficult to take a step back and address yourself to the question of whether or not you really need to move. However, now that we've seen just how much is involved in moving, it may well be worth reassessing the question. So, think hard about your reasons for moving and think carefully about how much it could cost you. If, for a modest outlay of less than £5 for this book, you come to the conclusion that there are cheaper alternatives, your investment will have been hugely rewarded by saving thousands of pounds, as well as time and energy.

Take a good look at your present home and make a list of all its good points, such as the location, the building, the size of rooms, the garden and what specially attracted you to your home in the first place. Clearly, there are often unavoidable reasons for moving, but some of us do move for reasons that are avoidable.

The one thing that you cannot change about your present home is its location. You can't take it somewhere else. However, many other things about it, which may have prompted you to think of moving, can be altered or coped with. If your home is too small, think about whether it is possible to build on an extension, to turn the loft into one or two rooms, to build a room on to the garage or on top of it or to split one large room into two smaller ones. If your home is too large, consider whether your money would be better spent by simply closing off one floor and turning off the radiators or perhaps by letting part of it.

If the problem is that you do not have a garage, see whether it is possible to build one by consulting an architect; alternatively, make enquiries about renting one nearby. It may be that it is the garden, or lack of one, that has made you wish to move. Clearly, if you do not have one, and you would like one, you will need to move – an allotment isn't always that satisfying. However, if the problem is that the garden is too large for you, you could spend up to £1000, say, and landscape it so that you are left with a compact garden to view from the house; the remainder can be allowed to run wild out of sight behind a pergola, trellis, wall or fence – or you could sell it.

What are known as 'amenities' are often the cause of people deciding to move – or, more likely, the lack of amenities. You may be too far from the children's schools, shops, a good library, or sporting facilities. If you still like your home and the area, however, you may be wiser to buy a car than to move.

Unavoidable moves

If you are contemplating moving because of your job, or that of your partner, to be nearer to the children's schools, because you need a larger house or garden, because you cannot bear the area or because of an impending divorce, you clearly have no alternative but to move.

Going ahead

Assuming that you are now firmly committed to moving, the next stage of this business venture is to rationalize some of the items in the fixed costs checklist above, aiming to keep your costs as low as possible. It is essential to make your budget as realistic as possible in order to work out just how much you can afford to spend on buying your new home. You should regard the money and the time you put into this venture as a substantial investment, probably the largest investment of money that you are ever likely to make. Making the right decision makes good business sense, and, because we are talking about your home, rather than just a building, this investment should bring rewards not only in financial terms in the future but also now in terms of your quality of life. A happy home should be a source of enjoyment rather than a source of continued anxiety. The fixed costs checklist above is intended to help you calculate how much you are able to spend. Let's look at some of the items in that checklist in greater detail.

Your surveyor

We are concerned here with whether or not to have a survey carried out and how to find a surveyor if you decide to go ahead.

Many people are tempted to save money by relying merely on the lender's valuation of the property. However, the lender is interested only in determining whether or not the property is worth approximately the asking price. The lender is not interested in faults or problems with the property that may prove both essential and expensive to remedy. The lender's valuation is often referred to as a survey, but it cannot, in practice, be regarded as such.

I recall a friend's case in 1984 in which the bank's surveyor (valuer) stated that the damp-proofing and electrical works had been carried out to a satisfactory standard. The buyer discovered soon after moving in that there was no damp-proofing, let alone any of a 'satisfactory standard', and the electrical works were declared 'unsafe' as none of the sockets had been earthed and the cable bringing the supply in from the street was of too small a gauge to be considered safe. The wretched buyer consulted a solicitor who put these and other matters to the valuer, who responded to a charge of negligence by drawing attention to the small print on the report: 'The valuer(s) has/have made this report without any acceptance of responsibility on his/their part to you'. The solicitor then informed the valuer that 'the ambit of these clauses is so wide that they cannot possibly be construed as "reasonable" within the meaning of the Unfair Contract Terms Act 1977'.

The buyer did not succeed in making the valuer accountable. The buyer commissioned a full structural surveyor's report some months *after* his purchase, in order to determine the scale of the problems. The surveyor concluded that there were a number of major defects with the building. The defects in question cost £14,000 to put right. Following new legal rulings in April 1989, today the buyer could confidently pursue the matter, provided he had the money with which to take his original surveyor to court.

The main point of this sorry tale is that the buyer decided in

May 1984 to save £200 plus VAT on a surveyor's report, saying, 'Well, the bank says it's all right'. In August 1984 he found that this saving was outweighed by having bought a defective property, which required some £12,000 to be spent as a matter of urgency and a further £2000 in the foreseeable future. So, regard the bank or building society's valuation simply as a document that satisfies the lender's purposes but is nothing to do with your decision to buy. Your budget should therefore include a sum for a surveyor's report.

The second point of this tale is that the valuer in question was also an estate agent. Surveying is a technical skill, while being an estate agent is a commercial and marketing skill, and it is debatable whether the two mix well. It is wise to choose someone who is a full-time working surveyor, rather than one who sells houses for a living and happens also to have the qualification to carry out a valuation now and again.

Finding a surveyor

The surest way to find a competent surveyor is on the personal recommendation of someone whose opinion you respect and who has no vested interest. Approaching a professional association is not the answer, as membership does not necessarily indicate professional competence. These associations often function as protective bodies for their members rather than as consumer watchdogs. Make sure that the person of your choice makes a full-time living from surveying. Ask for a quotation of charges and remember to add VAT at 15 per cent.

Essential building costs

The lender's valuation may include a note of works that are considered necessary. These can include substantial and serious things like remedying dry or damp rot, or comparatively insignificant items such as repainting the exterior window frames. The lender – your building society or bank – will almost certainly make it a condition of the mortgage that you carry out these works or, alternatively, they will withhold the amount required to carry them out until you have done so and their valuer has confirmed, for an additional fee, that you have done so satisfactorily.

At this point, you must sit down and think seriously about the nature of the defects and whether or not you still wish to proceed with buying the property. If you do, the next step is to acquire no fewer than three quotations for the work (remember VAT) and then decide whether or not your budget can stretch to it. If it cannot, and you feel that you are on quite firm ground with the vendors – in other words, they are relying upon you to buy their property, have shown no signs of gazumping and have not menaced you with hints about other buyers just waiting for the opportunity of stepping into your shoes – then approach them with a view to negotiating a reduction in the asking price (or approach their estate agent if you cannot face doing it yourself).

The most important thing of all is not to let yourself be carried away by the idea that this is the *one* property you really want. Remember we are looking at this as a business venture, and the transaction must make good financial sense. There will always be other, just as desirable, properties, so do keep your budget to the forefront of your mind and seek to reduce costs wherever possible.

Relocation agents

These agents 'relocate' you from one property to another, retaining an estate agent to sell your existing property, lining up suitable properties for you to view in accordance with a detailed description of what you are looking for, get the survey done, raise the finance and see through the entire negotiation. They charge 1–1½ per cent of the purchase price of your new property, plus VAT at 15 per cent.

There is one significant drawback to using a relocation firm however. You will have given them a description of the type of house you are looking for, together with a list of essential features. If the agent views a property that lacks a feature you have defined as essential or that has something about it that you have already indicated would rule out a positive choice, you may not be invited to see it. However, it may be that the house is so charming and exactly what you want in all but this one respect that had you been house-hunting yourself, you might have come to the conclusion that you would be prepared to compromise on this one consideration.

You have, therefore, to weigh this potential drawback against the fact that such agents can save you a great deal of time if you simply need a place to live, rather than a home to love, and you are not overly concerned with a very detailed specification.

Relocation agents normally only accept commissions in which the purchaser is seeking to buy at over £150,000, as the fee would not meet their time on lower-priced properties.

Relocation agents have come into existence chiefly to make up for the awesome deficiencies of estate agents, who typically bombard a prospective purchaser with details of properties that are totally unsuitable whether in terms of price, location or accommodation.

When you set out your budget, you need to calculate whether it makes good financial sense to retain a relocation agent. For example, if you can get time off work without losing pay, or if you are not working, you will probably not need one. But, if you are self-employed, and you are therefore going to lose time and money in house-hunting and seeing through the negotiations, you need to work out which is the greater: income lost through doing it yourself, or the agent's fee. As a rule of thumb, you will generally benefit financially from retaining a relocation agent only if you are earning more than £15,000 per year. If, for example, you and your partner's income, as self-employed people, amounts to £50 per hour, you can save by using a professional relocator. To demonstrate this, let's say you're looking for a property at £200,000. You'd have to pay the agent £2000 plus VAT (=£2300). Let's say the amount of time involved is 60 hours (spread out over perhaps four months). If both you and your partner are involved, the negotiation will cost £3000 of your time, but an agent would cost £2300. You may also be able to offset a proportion of the fee against tax, if you work from home.

This boils down to saving some £700 if the estimated number of hours is correct. As I've already said, however, if you have an understanding employer, or you are not currently working, do it yourself. (The services offered by relocation agents are discussed in more detail in Chapter 2. If choosing one, remember that a personal recommendation is desirable.)

Selling your own home

Very few people think that the estate agents who handled the sale of their property had earned their fee. You may feel that you would prefer to market and sell your existing property yourself. This takes time, however, and a knowledge of what to do and what not to do. It should be said, however, that selling your home still takes time, even if you do use an estate agent, but perhaps not as long. As with relocation agents, you need to calculate the *relative* costs of your loss of income if you decide to market and sell your home compared with the saving made on the estate agent's fee.

Let's say your £100,000 home is to be sold on a joint agency basis of a fee of 2 per cent of the selling price. The estate agent who sells it will charge £2000 plus VAT (=£2300). If your house is sold for £250,000, the agent will invoice you for £5000 plus VAT (=£5750). If you continue to work, can you match this sum? If you are not working, or you work on a temporary or freelance basis, you can probably make more selling your property yourself than you can commissioning someone else to do it, while continuing with your own work . . . provided *only* that you know how to do it, what the pitfalls are, and how to avoid them:

1 You will need to have the house professionally valued by three independent valuers, who will each charge at least £100 or more plus VAT at 15 per cent.
2 You will have to produce publicity material, including good photographs.

3 You will need to make sure that this material reaches a good number of serious prospective purchasers.
4 You will need a permanently manned telephone, or one with an answering machine/service.
5 You need to know how to follow up an expression of interest or a firm offer by a prospective purchaser and some skill or experience in negotiating.
6 You will need a good solicitor, to whom you can turn things over at the earliest possible opportunity.

If you think that this is something you can do, obtain a copy of *Bradshaw's Guide to Marketing Your House* (published by Castle Books in 1983) from your local lending library, quoting the Dewey reference number 333.33, before you make your final decision. There's no doubt that you *could* save a very large sum of money by selling your house yourself, but establish what is involved first. It could take anything from 12 hours, if you are lucky, to 40 hours or more.

A solicitor or a conveyancer?

Conveyancing, in which a property is legally conveyed from one person to another, can be carried out by a solicitor or by a licensed conveyancer. Conveyancers are normally cheaper than solicitors, but they will not usually have such wide training and experience in law. This means that if complicated problems present themselves, you may need to seek professional clarification from a solicitor; at worst, a conveyancer could overlook a fine point. If the property concerned is a flat, or if it is a leasehold property, both of which can involve more complex legalities, I would recommend a solicitor. If you do use a conveyancer check that he or she is licensed.

If you decide upon a solicitor, make sure that he or she regularly carries out conveyancing and establish what his or her fees (not forgetting VAT at 15 per cent) are to be. You do not need to use a family solicitor in London's Gray's Inn Square or a comparable smart location. Try to find a good high street solicitor on personal recommendation from someone who has used the firm recently.

The legal system of England and Wales differs from that of Scotland: if you, for example, sell in England and buy in Scotland, you will need two solicitors – one who is qualified to practise in England and Wales, and a second who practises in Scottish law.

When you speak to a prospective solicitor, you could ask, by way of a test of competence, what charges you are likely to be involved in throughout the transaction. Check off what you are told against the fixed costs checklist on pages 7–11 to make sure that the solicitor knows the business and to check that there is no *new* or other law, fee or charge which will affect your budget.

Regular outgoings

We are concerned here, principally, with mortgage repayments, general rates and water rate, and any service charge that may be applied to flats or communal gardens. Ideally, your monthly mortgage repayment should be no more than one-quarter of your monthly income, both sums to be calculated *after* tax and referred to, therefore, as *net* rather than gross. In practice, you should be able to manage a repayment that constitutes one-third of your income. However, if the monthly repayment is near or close to half of your monthly income, you will undoubtedly find it difficult to manage, and you would be wise not to undertake such a large commitment unless you are absolutely certain that your income is to rise, substantially, in the near future.

A building society or bank will provide you with a list of figures showing the monthly repayments on the different types of mortgage for the loan you have in mind, both net and gross. If they stress the *net* figure, ask them at what rate they have computed tax, and thus tax relief, and make sure it tallies with *your* tax rate.

It is most important not to overstretch yourself, because if anything goes wrong with the house, *and* interest rates rise, thus causing your repayments to increase, you may not be able to cope and may therefore have to sell the property, with all the associated costs – and you will still need somewhere to live.

The rates are simple to ascertain. Ask the vendor or the estate agent for the rateable value of the property and also ask what rate in the pound is charged by the relevant local council. If you are told that the rateable value is £400 and the rate in the pound is £2, you will know that the yearly rates are £800. Most councils allow you to pay this by regular standing order. (From April 1990 (April 1989 in Scotland) rates will be phased out and the community charge, or 'poll tax', a *fixed* amount which every adult – with a few exceptions – will have to pay, will be phased in.) There will also be a water rate, which in large cities does not usually amount to a substantial sum. In rural areas, however, the water rate can be a significant figure in calculating your budget.

Have we thought of everything?

Probably not, but it must be said that it is important, in one sense, *not* to take absolutely everything into account when buying a home, particularly if you are a first-time buyer. For example, if you made a budget incorporating almost all of the thirteen items in the fixed cost checklist on pages 7–11 and then added a cooker, fridge, china, cutlery, pans, furniture, carpets, curtains, bedlinen, towels and doormat, you would quite likely find that you could not afford to buy a home at all. What's crucial is striking the balance between those items that you *have* to pay for and those you need plus those you would like – ideally. It is nevertheless essential to formulate a realistic budget to include items 1–4, 7 (possibly) and 8–13 from the fixed cost checklist, together with those items from the additional costs checklist on page 22 that you know you cannot do without. Remember, when you're going through this second checklist, that things can sometimes be done cheaply at the start. (Buy a microwave for your first year instead of hob and oven, a second-hand fridge and essential furniture from second-hand shops or local ads, for example. See Chapter 5 for more about doing things cheaply.)

Additional costs

These include:

1 Any costs incurred to make up for lost time in conveyancing, for example a private search fee or couriers for documents, when any delay could cause you to lose the property, having already incurred surveyor's and solicitor's fees.
2 Building works you may feel the need to carry out as indicated by your surveyor's report.
3 Specialist surveys recommended by the surveyor's report. These can include specialist reports on drains, electrics, rising damp, or dry rot, for example.
4 Building projects that you would like to have done (knocking two rooms in to one, for example).
5 Cupboards and shelving.
6 Decorating.
7 Carpeting or other flooring.
8 Curtains.
9 Furniture, particularly for the first-time buyer, who may have to invest in a cooker and fridge, for example.
10 The so-called little things that can start to add up – doorbell, power points, towel rails, loo roll holder, mirrors, and many more.

You may feel that these are things you either do not need, or can manage without. They are just examples, however, the point being that you should be prepared for unforeseen expenses and you would be wise to allow a contingency figure for these in your budget.

Adding it all up

If you work systematically through the fixed costs and additional costs checklists you should be able to arrive at an informed estimate of what it will cost you to move house. When you want to fix your price range for house-hunting, bear in mind how much money you have set by; how much you will receive for your existing property, after clearing the outstanding mortgage; the costs of moving; and the amount a building society or bank is prepared to lend you.

Try to stick to your budget as closely as possible, without being completely inflexible, and try to make sure that you sell your present home for what it is worth and that you find a new home within your price range. House-hunting is the subject of the next chapter.

Will I survive?

I have painted what I hope is a realistic picture, rather than an unusually pessimistic one, of the costs associated with moving house so that you can work out a thoroughly practical budget and not be floored by an unexpected expense. Moving house is undoubtedly expensive and troublesome, but take encouragement from the fact that over 60 per cent of us own our own homes and that most home-owners move more than once in their lives. It often seems awful at the time, but you can be reasonably sure that the horror of it will dissipate within a year or two of the move – after which you can start to enjoy your large investment.

2

House-hunting

Before you go out to look for a new home, you must know how much money you have available to spend, as discussed in the previous chapter. Once you have established this, the next thing to do is to think about exactly what you are looking for. Take a look at the list on page 26, then make your own list of the essential features of your new home, in order of their importance to *you*. Your list will stand you in good stead if and when you start to feel exhausted or bored with house-hunting: just sit back, take a deep breath and think, 'Well, I haven't actually seen what I'm looking for yet, so I'll carry on . . . I'm not going to buy something that I don't like or is unsuitable.'

One of the most important things to remember when you are house-hunting is not to become so overwhelmed by predatory estate agents and your own fatigue that you end up buying a home about which you may later on hear yourself saying, 'Well, it's not really what we had in mind but we quite like it now', or, 'We simply ran out of time and energy to go out looking any more.'

Some friends of mine moved from a Surrey commuter town to what they thought was a pleasant Sussex town. Soon after they moved they discovered that the entire town for a ten-mile radius was the subject of planning agreements for light industrial units. The surrounding countryside was being carved up faster than cake. These people moved again, within a year, further south . . . so in two years they were paying for a double lot of moving costs. So it's important to take a good look not only at what you intend to buy but also at the surrounding area.

In another case a friend bought an elegant Georgian house in a pleasant tree-lined street in South London. He hadn't really noticed the pub four doors down and so he did not visit the area at closing time to see if there would be a problem with noise. If he had, he would have discovered what he found out only after he had moved in: closing time was typically followed by screams of laughter in the street, the occasional obstreperous drunk, the screech of tyres – and a litter of junk food wrappers to greet him in the front garden each morning. All this may well not have put him off the house, but at least he would have been aware of it.

I saw a house myself in spring 1987, again an elegant Georgian house facing the heath at Blackheath in London, in a rather dilapidated condition. I wondered why all the windows were not only double glazed but also permanently sealed. I went over there one evening and visited a nearby pub – which was holding one of its regular twice-weekly music nights which made it all too clear why local inhabitants would want to keep their windows closed.

Again in spring 1987 I went to look at a house in Sussex and in the short space of the 20 minutes that I was there noticed a plane or two flying overhead. 'Oh yes,' said the vendor breezily, 'we do get the occasional plane over on a Sunday.' On checking with Gatwick I found that the house was under the main flight path, and that they considered a Sunday afternoon in April not to be a busy time! I remember, too, looking at a flat some years ago in the Clapham area of London and wondering what the strange rumbling and shaking in the flat could be caused by. The flat was but a stone's throw from Clapham Junction, which could have been convenient in some ways but perhaps not in others.

As I said in Chapter 1, the one thing you cannot do to your home is literally move it, so, for that reason, the location is almost always the first consideration and the most important one. Where it is located is something that you cannot afford to compromise upon, for that is where you will be living. With this in mind, you should give some thought to the local bus, tube and rail services, unless you intend to travel, without exception, by car.

What you are looking for

Take a look at the list below and then make your own, placing the most important consideration at the top:

1 Where is it to be?
2 Do you want a flat or a house?
3 How many bedrooms do you want?
4 How many reception rooms?
5 Do you need more than one bathroom?
6 Do you want a fully fitted kitchen with spaces to take your own equipment?
7 What age or style of home do you want – medieval, Georgian, Victorian, Edwardian, twenties, thirties, forties, fifties, sixties, or modern (that is, less than 20 years old)?
8 Do you want a yard, patio or garden? If you want a garden, should it, in estate agent's jargon, be 'compact and easily maintained' (up to 30 feet long), good (up to 60 ft), large (up to 100 ft), very large (up to 200 ft), or larger still? For gardens greater than about 200 ft in length, or measuring more than about one-fifth of an acre, estate agents give their size in acres.
9 Do you want a garage, or a double garage?
10 Do you want a 'modernized' property, that is, one with central heating?
11 Are you looking for an old and untouched property which you can rescue and restore to its former beauty?
12 What sort of amenities do you need, such as ease of travel to your place of work, the children's schools and the shops?

Make your own list of the essential features of your new home and the surrounding area, in order of their importance to *you*.

Before you start looking

Once you have your priorities clearly ordered, you are almost ready to start looking. But, first, you need to satisfy yourself on two important counts:
1 You can raise the money for what you need, probably in the form of a mortgage unless you are in the fortunate position of being a cash buyer.

2 You will be able to sell your existing home, unless of course you are a first-time buyer.

This raises the very tricky question of whether to try to sell your home first, at least to the stage of a firm offer and then to look; or to find something you like and then set about selling your existing home. And, of course, money is the root of the problem.

Raising the money

Some people believe that it is best to find the property you want and only then to consult your building society or bank. Others, myself included, believe it is better to consult potential lenders first (see *Getting advice about a mortgage* in Chapter 3) and establish a few ground rules. These include:

- the amount of money they will lend
- the age of properties for which they are prepared to grant a mortgage (some won't lend on anything older than Victorian, others don't like lending on flat conversions)
- the condition of the property
- their views on freeholds and leaseholds.

Once you have obtained a preliminary, theoretical go-ahead from the lender, you can at least, even if you have not sold your existing property, tell the estate agent and the vendor that 'There's no problem with a mortgage – I've already been into that.' Clearly, the vendor and his estate agent will smile upon you if you are additionally able to say, truthfully, 'Yes, I can get the mortgage and the sale of my own house is already well advanced.' This is the tricky bit. You obviously cannot lie about it, if only because you will soon be found out.

When should you start selling?

If you start selling before you have found anywhere that you like, you have to run the risk of settling for something that may not be quite what you wanted in order not to lose the sale of your current home. If, on the other hand, you find somewhere you like first, the worst that can happen is that either you receive less for your existing home than you'd hoped (for a 'quick sale') or you may need a bridging loan until the sale of your current home has caught up with the purchase of your new one. Bridging loans are to be avoided as far as possible, but it does sometimes pay to use this expensive form of finance to tide you over.

A couple of years ago some elderly friends of mine started to look around at what was on the market in the way of sheltered accommodation. It so happened that they were shown a quite remarkable flat, one of a small number of good quality conversions from a large Georgian house in Bath with resident warden and other essential facilities. There were only three on the market, they knew that they would be unlikely to find anything as pleasant elsewhere, as they had already seen a number of others, and the price was comparatively reasonable. They had not put their house on the market but they decided to go ahead in any case and take the risk. They did eventually sell their house, at the most difficult time of year – in the winter, but not before they had shown no less than 40 prospective buyers around and paid for bridging finance for four months. They knew that this was the right decision and they have not regretted it, even though they had to bridge for £110,000 for four months – which probably cost well over £4000, perhaps nearer £5000, in interest payments. In their case, they were selling for more than they were buying and could therefore take the risk. Not all of us can.

So, weighing up which to do first, it's money versus quality: either look first and find what you like, and perhaps accept less on your sale; or start selling first and then look, perhaps having to settle for less than the perfect property. The other, final point to bear in mind in this tricky equation is this: the vendor of the place you go for is practically certain to choose the buyer who has arranged a mortgage and whose sale is under way. If you admit that your sale is not under way, and the property not even on the market, the vendor will rightly feel anxious. After all, he or she has no idea of how saleable your property is and therefore what time scale is involved. As I said, it's tricky.

There are two possible solutions to the problem. The first is preparing to sell your house, without actually taking it to the point where it is on the market (as described below). The second solution, which often does work out, is to hope that the vendor's buyer's own sale falls through and that the vendor will come back to you in a few weeks. This is exactly what happened to us in 1987 – although by then we had changed our minds about the house anyway! (That happens quite a lot, too, so don't be despondent, if you don't secure your first choice: you are certain to find something better in the end.)

My mother is a great advocate of finding the right house first and in 1959, after a search of no less than three years, found a beautiful but dilapidated house going for a song. No mortgage company would touch it, but my parents arranged private finance. They then put their current house on the market and, in the time it took to sell, they were gazumped and lost the beautiful house. My mother could not find anything else to compare, so, rather than give up the sale on the existing house, she arranged to move a family of five with an au pair, a dog, a cat and a parrot, into a flat as a temporary measure. She had to take out a five-year lease on the flat and, just as she had done so, the owner of the beautiful house came back and reoffered her the house. Of course she took it – and sublet the flat for four and a half years. However, a lot of us would regard this tale as a warning to sell first. My view is 'prepare to sell'.

Preparing to sell

Just before you start looking, think about how you are going to sell your house. Are you going to do it yourself, or are you going to retain one or more estate agents? If you intend to do it yourself, go ahead with the first two stages described in the previous chapter (valuations and producing the publicity material). If you are to use an estate agent, decide how many and who, have them around to value the house and make up their description of it. Ask to see the description when it is ready and check that it is more or less accurate. In this way, they only have to do the mail-out when you give the word rather than starting from scratch.

How many agents?

If you retain one agent and give him exclusive rights to sell, his commission will be lower. If you use two or more, it may be as much as double the commission, but, between them, they will reach more, although not double the number, of prospective purchasers.

If you use a sole agent, you grant sole agency; do not, under any circumstances, grant 'sole selling rights' as this means that you must pay the agent the commission even if you happen to sell the house yourself to a friend or acquaintance. Commission varies from 1½ per cent to 3, depending on whether it is a sole, joint or multiple agency; where the property is; what it is worth. By all means try and negotiate a reduction in the commission figure. If it is a 'low' time of year, such as winter, the agent may agree. He is unlikely to agree in spring and early summer when he probably has plenty of houses to sell.

Finding your new home

So, armed with a note of your maximum figure and a list of those features you consider essential, it's time to think about where and how best to look for your new home. Several options will present themselves and, in my view, it is worth using all of them:

1 Estate agents (they charge the vendor, not you as the buyer). In Scotland you may buy and sell through solicitors' property centres.
2 Property shops (particularly for lower-priced properties, but you can expect even less of a personal service than from agents).
3 The local newspaper (in which you will find advertisements both by agents and by private vendors).
4 'For Sale' boards outside a house – walk or drive around the

area in which you hope to buy and make a note of the telephone number on the board.

5 Word of mouth – tell as many people as possible in the area that you are hoping to move and what you are looking for.

6 Relocation agents – who will get everything that you could get yourself from estate agents, sift through the details, discard all those that are patently unsuitable, view a select number and report back to you with their opinions. Once the sale has gone through, they will charge you a commission of perhaps 1½ per cent. They will usually act for you only if you seek to buy at over £150,000.

Using an estate agent

This is what most people do, and it is this side of an estate agent's work that attracts the fiercest criticism. An estate agent acts for the vendor, with the intention of selling their property for him or her. He does not act for a prospective buyer, has no loyalty to any particular buyer, and regards buyers only as useful instruments in obtaining his commission for the sale of the property registered on his books *by the vendor*.

Be sure to bear all this in mind at all times, and, therefore, never believe anything an estate agent tells you unless you can obtain independent corroboration.

Visit the agents of your choice in the area, ideally on a weekday. Saturday is their busiest day, and it is also the day that the offices are manned by temporary staff, some of whom may not work there during the week. Tell them what you are looking for, but do not expect them to take in anything other than the price range quoted. They will then hand you a sheaf of particulars of properties in that price range, without making any distinction about the individual features of any particular property. Read through the lot, checking off the features mentioned in the description against your own list of essential features. If any property appears to conform with what you are looking for, ask to view it. Do not agree to view something that is in the wrong area, is too expensive for you, lacks the garden you consider essential or is, in some way, totally unsuitable. Agents will typically try and try to make you see properties that are nothing like what you want in the hope that you will soon be worn down by the search and make an offer on a shack. This is why you drew up a list of features your new home must have – always keep this list in mind.

As I have said, agents act for the vendor and, to that end, will do everything in their power to sell the property without actually tying up a prospective purchaser and forging their signature.

You may find it odd, particularly if you are a first-time buyer, to be presented with details of properties that are clearly unsuitable. However, it is quicker for the agent to have someone photocopy a sheet of particulars 100 or 200 times than it is for him to deal with each buyer on a personal basis and systematically go through the properties on his books with the intention of identifying the two or three that are probably what you want. Agents defend their way of working by claiming that 'People hardly ever actually buy what they say they are looking for.' This is hardly surprising, since the fatigue engendered by reading the fine details within the particulars (including the number of power points) about a large number of quite unsuitable properties and even having to see some of these places, militates against finding the right place. You may have given up and settled for something different before it actually comes on to the market.

So, try not to become frustrated and tired of dealing with estate agents, because the majority of houses and flats for sale are on their books – you need them as much as they need you. Try instead to be highly selective and refuse politely to view properties you consider unsuitable, giving your reasons. The agent will then try to make you reconsider: don't listen, just repeat, 'No, I think not, thank you.' Be firm: agents understand the spoken word quite well. Be civilized: remember you will need them on your side when at last you strike and make an offer on something. If you refuse to see unsuitable properties and always give your reasons for turning down something you have seen, the agent will at least know that your intentions are serious when you do make an offer. If you refuse to see anything without being able to state your reasons, the agent may begin to wonder if you are serious. Equally, if you do view, always report back to the agent as soon as possible, ideally the same day, with a 'Yes' or a 'No' plus your reasons. If you say 'No', don't allow yourself to be talked into reconsidering or making a second viewing. Remember, when you do see what you want, you will know straightaway that this is The One.

Estate agents' descriptions

I noted just now that agents mostly understand the spoken word quite well, but they are a little less reliable on the written word. Some of the phrases and odd linguistic touches that distinguish estate agents' essays about the properties they are intent upon selling are now instantly recognizable. Always remember as you read an estate agent's description of a house that he is trying to sell you something, just as a car salesman is. Any good points of the house (or car) will therefore be praised lavishly, while the bad points will be ignored. If you happen to raise a potentially bad point, the salesman or agent may look at you with an air of astonishment. Remember, too, that what you intend to spend on buying a home will be many times more than the amount you would spend on buying a car, so do take that much more care – and take the salesman's embellishments with a pinch of salt.

The estate agent's description of a property will include:

- a note of the asking price
- a description of the location and any amenities
- a description of the property itself, and whether it is freehold or leasehold, followed by a detailed description room by room
- a description of the garden
- a note of the rateable value (you need the latter in order to work out what the yearly rates would be, as described in Chapter 1).

The asking price

A property is worth what someone will pay for it, no more. This means that if a property is on the market for an unusually long time (over four or five months) it is not worth the price asked. If it were, someone would have bought it. So, try and establish at the outset how long the property has been on the market; if it has been for sale for two or three months, you stand a good chance of buying the property for less than the price specified.

Some properties are marked 'Quick sale' with the implication that the price has been fixed low in order to get this quick sale. However, this is sometimes just a marketing ploy to encourage people to believe that they are getting a bargain – so beware. Once you have looked at up to a dozen properties, you will have an idea of what a property is worth and the reasons why one may be more expensive than another. A property is sometimes marked 'Vacant possession', which means that it is empty or about to be, and that you need not worry about the vendor having to find a new home before you can proceed with your purchase. Lastly, you can sometimes negotiate on the price of a house, depending on the price range and the condition of the property, how quickly the vendor wishes to secure a sale and how long the property has been on the market.

Most properties in Scotland are offered at an asking or 'upset' price but some are marketed at a fixed price.

Describing the location

The estate agent will probably offer an exaggerated view of the area in which the property is located. Agents are not accountable for the accuracy of their descriptions, and you should check the local amenities yourself. Familiarize yourself with the area by walking around it at different times of day.

A house in South London, for example, was described by several agents as being within minutes of Denmark Hill Station 'offering fast and frequent services to both the City and West End'. In reality, the house was an uphill walk of a minimum of ten minutes (provided you were fit) from the station in question; the services to the City were in fact slow and infrequent and only ran during the rush-hour periods; and there were no services to the West End.

You also need to know, particularly in rural areas, how far away the station is: '28 minutes to Waterloo or 50 minutes to Victoria', for example, is not quite what it seems if you discover it takes 20 minutes to drive to the station, and the station car park charges are so excessive that you cannot afford them anyway.

'Convenient for' can disguise a variety of sins. 'Convenient for motorway', for example, may mean that it is close enough for you to hear the roar of the traffic day and night but it may also turn out that there is no exit anywhere near your house and is not, therefore, in any practical sense, convenient. 'Conveniently located to good schools', again, can mean anything, depending on your views. Some people believe that state schools are 'good', while others would rate only private/public schools 'good'. The proximity of a school can, in addition, mean noise, particularly if the school has a large playground and playing fields, and it may also mean youthful vandalism in the area. 'Convenient for shops' depends on what sort of shops you find useful. The 'shops' in question may turn out to be one antique shop and one water-bed shop. If you want to know what's convenient, therefore, to any property you're interested in, do walk around the area, have a drink in the local pub and buy the local newspaper. Gather as much information as you can.

Freehold or leasehold?

Most houses, although not all, are sold on a 'freehold' basis, which means that the property belongs to you, once any loan or mortgage has been paid off. Most flats, however, though not all, are sold on a 'leasehold' basis: this means that you will never actually own the flat but that you own the lease to it and you can sell the lease when you wish to move once again.

Buying and selling leasehold properties is usually more complicated than buying and selling freeholds and you are therefore recommended to retain a solicitor for these transactions.

The length of the lease is one of the crucial factors. The shorter a lease is, the less value it has. Flat buyers should be particularly aware of this: a surprisingly reasonably priced flat may, for example, only have 30 years left on the lease. In fashionable areas of London, it is by no means unusual to see flats advertised for many thousands of pounds – for an eight- or ten-year lease. You may be sure that it will be difficult, if not impossible, to raise a mortgage on such properties. Firstly, mortgage terms are not usually shorter than ten years. Secondly, some lenders insist that there must remain 40 unexpired years on the lease after the mortgage has been cleared. If you are seeking a 25-year mortgage, therefore, you will need to find a property whose lease is at least 65 years.

Houses that are sold leasehold tend to have long leases attached (90 years or more) and are often renewable. Your solicitor will be able to advise you about the implications of a particular lease upon a particular property. In Scotland, long leases are rather unusual.

Owners of leasehold properties commonly have to meet outgoings that freeholders do not: for example, a ground rent until the lease runs out may be payable and there may also be charges for 'services' and further charges for maintenance of 'common' areas – for example, the roof, and exterior brickwork and paintwork. These charges can amount to a considerable sum and they may also increase from year to year; if you are looking at such properties, therefore, be sure to make detailed enquiries about recurring costs and liabilities and have your solicitor, at pre-contract stage, check the terms of the lease. Leaseholders have some rights, which your solicitor would be able to clarify in respect of a particular lease, in that they may inspect the accounts that relate to recurring costs and they may be offered the right to purchase a freehold share in the property should the freehold ownership change hands.

Describing the property

First, regard the word 'style' when used by an estate agent with the utmost suspicion.

'Georgian style in private road' actually describes a completely modern house with a reproduction Georgian façade and situated on a housing estate.

'Tudor-style' means any half-timbered building constructed from the 1930s onwards. 'Swedish-style' may mean it looks like a hut such as you might see in the northern fir forests.

'Architect-styled' often means that the entire ground floor is open plan and the staircase open tread, making the house less than ideal for noisy children – or for their parents, anyway.

'Cottage-style' means a house that is ancient, poky, dark, with minute rooms and ceilings so low that the owner has developed a permanent stoop.

'Conceived with some style', 'fitted out with style' or 'stylish' usually indicate that the owner has been rash enough to put his or her individual hallmark on the property, and only you will know if you consider it stylish – or abominable.

'Family house', a phrase used to describe anything with more than two bedrooms, is entirely meaningless. Only you can decide if it is a house suited to your family.

Any reference to 'atmosphere' should be ignored: 'warm and relaxed atmosphere' could well mean the house is filthy and the dogs are completely out of control.

If you are looking for a property of a particular period, ask the agent the date of the building, and make sure that he gives you a precise date. He can get this information from the owner, who will know it from the deeds. 'It looks quite mellow/old/character-ful' are typical agent responses best ignored.

The description may make some reference to the size of the property, but if it does not you may assume that it is tiny. 'Compact' in agents' terms means that even a cat would protest that it felt cramped. 'Easily maintained' means it is very small, usually with perfectly square or rectangular rooms – no interest-ing bits and no 'decorative features' – which usually means picture rails, moulded ceilings, turned banisters, archways, window seats and so forth. 'Deceptively spacious' means it looks small but you will be amazed to see that the owner has fitted in essentials such as cooking equipment, something to sit on and something to sleep on. When you look at a property for yourself, remember one vital point: empty rooms look *much* bigger. If the property is still lived in and looks spacious to you, then it is probably big enough. If it's empty, it should look *very* spacious to you.

A 'studio flat' conjures up visions of a large airy studio with a bedroom somewhere else until you know that 'studio flat' is the smallest property you can buy. The sitting room, bedroom, workroom and kitchen are all in the same room; the shower and loo are normally separate, but may not be entirely so.

Estate agents' descriptions are sometimes so ludicrously 'inexact' that they do, at least, provide some comic relief during the house-hunting process. If you start to feel that this is what you need, obtain a copy of *The Extremely Serious Guide to Moving House* by Keith Ray (Columbus Books 1987). Ray identifies, with a degree of exaggeration, some of the traps for the unwary – 'individual' meaning that 'the architect was shot after it was built to ensure he could never make the same sort of mistake again'; 'unexpectedly reavailable' meaning that 'the last buyer found out just in time'; 'within stone's throw of local schools' meaning that 'half the windows are broken every month'; and, on the subject of photographs of the property, 'the house is shown in a snowy setting but the details are sent out in August . . . one of the best indicators of what estate agents call a non-rapidly advancing purchase situation scenario'. If you are viewing in May or June, as many people do, beware properties photographed with bare-leaved trees or daffodils at their peak.

The interior

After a description of the property and the area in which it is located come the fine details, a room by room description of the property. The vital thing to watch for here is the oblique stroke: a kitchen/dining room, study/formal dining room/playroom, sitting room/conservatory means just three distinct rooms. The agent means that you can sit and eat in the kitchen if you wish; that you can use the dining room to eat in or you can turn it into a study or playroom; the sitting room has been built on afterwards in the form of a conservatory. What this sort of description does not mean is that there are seven rooms as well as the bedrooms. There's no doubt, however, that people are taken in again and again by this type of description, and lured to see what they imagine to be a mansion.

Do not rely on room measurements. Agents habitually tell straightforward untruths on this one, and add a few inches/feet to the dimensions of each room. 15'3" often actually means 14'6". 9'2" has been known to measure, in fact, 8'4". If you would like to know what the rooms measure, you have no alternative but to ask the owner if you may measure them. This is particularly important with small bedrooms, for example, when you need to know if your bed can be fitted in. Equally, if you want to fit in a table tennis table into a 'family' room or playroom, you must check the measurements, allowing plenty of space for movement around the table.

Estate agents' details are useful for the following: price, location, number of rooms (subject to oblique strokes) and some indication of the outdoors.

Before I deal with gardens, one note about bathrooms. 'Suite' means the lavatory, basin and bath. 'Lemon' indicates that those are in yellow, so does 'primrose'. 'Avocado' means that they are in the colour of pea soup. 'Plum', 'burgundy', 'claret' all mean deep red maroon. 'Midnight' means dark blue. 'Terracotta' means a light russet brown. Other more fanciful terms have to be seen to be believed. If a shower exists, check that it works: ask the vendor if you may turn it on to check that the water pressure is sufficient to make it work, explaining that you once bought a property with two showers, neither of which would work and produced no more than puzzled frowns from a succession of plumbers.

Outdoors

Estate agents' descriptions of gardens were mentioned at the start of this chapter in point 8 under 'What you are looking for'. Remember that 'compact and easily maintained' means it is very small indeed; a garden in Hampstead described in this way was just wide enough to take the width of the mower (14 inches). Any garden that is more than one-fifth of an acre will be described in terms of its acreage. A smaller garden will be described in feet, but again do not rely on an estate agent's dexterity with the measuring tape.

A garden in South London, which I know well, has been described by three agents as (1) '70 to 80 foot south west facing garden'; (2) '80 foot west facing garden'; (3) '110 foot south facing garden'. If it matters, measure it yourself and also determine which way it faces by locating it on a map of the area.

'Laid to lawn' means there is grass. 'Entirely laid to lawn' can mean that there are no flower beds and no shrubs. 'Paved for easy maintenance' means the grass has been concreted over.

'Well-stocked' means that there are some flower beds and plants. 'Mature' means that the garden is overrun with weeds and ancient shrubs which may have to be replaced very soon. 'Plenty of scope' means that nothing whatsoever has been done and it is up to you to create the garden in the space available. 'Ideal for children' means the same.

'Small, elegant patio' means that there is a back yard just large enough to accommodate you and two friends with a glass of wine. 'Communal gardens' means that you share the gardens with owners of adjacent properties; it does not mean that your property has direct access to the garden. You may have to go out of your front door, taking with you a key to the garden so that you may let yourself in and lock up afterwards. If there is direct access, the agent will be sure to say so on the particulars. If there is no mention of a garden, patio or even back yard, then there isn't one.

As always, beware the salesman's love of exaggeration: 'idyllic' means that it is really quite pleasant; 'delightful' means OK; 'pleasant' means utterly boring and bland and the owners loathe gardening; 'ideal for the gardening enthusiast' means that you will be starting from scratch, removing the builders' rubble. This type of exaggeration applies just as much to the property itself, so that something that is really quite awful can be described as 'pleasant' while anything of a reasonable size finds itself termed 'huge'/'magnificent'/'majestic'/'imposing'.

Not quite what we were expecting

You will have read enough by now to understand why house-hunting is tiring. Our expectations are raised so high, to be dashed so brutally by looking at the subject of the agent's description. We can learn several things from all this:

1 Don't expect anything to be marvellous. Imagine that every expedition will end in disappointment. Don't, whatever you do, get excited about any property that you are about to go and see, otherwise the frequent disappointments will soon make you feel that what you are looking for does not exist. Once you start believing this, you will feel tempted to go for something that isn't really what you want. And this is the basis of agents' claims that 'many people buy something totally different from what they said they wanted'.

2 When you are in the situation of being the vendor yourself, remember what house-hunting is like. First, check the agent's details for their accuracy so that people's expectations aren't raised to a ridiculous degree. An agent, for example, will happily describe a clothes peg as a cloakroom (yes, it has been known) and wonder why the viewers were annoyed or disappointed! Secondly, if the prospective buyers seem at all interested, offer them a cup of tea and place an ashtray in a visible position. Although you may dislike the smoking habit, a prospective buyer who is dying for a cigarette is not a happy person. In other words, do what you can to make prospective buyers feel at ease but do not put them under any pressure. They'll get plenty of that from your agent. If you are showing your home to a couple, leave them alone for a short while with the words, 'You'd probably like to have a look round on your own.'

3 As a prospective buyer, you can reduce the number of places you see by using a relocation agent, but this will cost you 1–1½ per cent plus VAT on top of the purchase price and usually applies only to properties over £150,000, as the commission would not be high enough to make it worth the agent's while to look for lower-priced properties.

41

Taking the pain out of looking

Apart from not pegging your hopes too high, there are a number of things to bear in mind when you are house-hunting, which may make the whole process easier and more efficient:

1 Give yourself enough time. Make up your mind that this is your current priority and that the other things you normally do in your spare time have to take second place. Don't try and sandwich a visit between finishing work and going out unless it's unavoidable.

2 Try and see each place for the first time in daylight. You can always take your second viewing after dark when you want to confirm that this really is The One. There is much you miss when you view in the dark – particularly the area and the immediate outdoors – so try to make the first visit in the daylight hours if at all possible.

3 If two of you are house-hunting together, and one is much keener to move and also much choosier about where to move to, let that one be the person to make the first viewing. Only involve the partner for the second viewing, in order that a degree of enthusiasm can be maintained and only one person's time wasted on unsuitable properties.

4 Try if you possibly can to have a friend look after your children. Most children find house-hunting very tedious and have no qualms about showing it. This means it's difficult to maintain a conversation with your partner and difficult sometimes even to keep a picture of the property in your mind. Take them along for any second viewing, if you are definitely interested in the property, if you feel that the children should be able to express their opinion about where the family is to live.

5 Restrict yourself to seeing no more than two properties in an evening or five (at the very most) in an entire day. If you see too many, you are likely to become confused and exhausted.

6 If you arrange to see several, try to organize the day so that you can have a pub lunch and a break for a cup of tea in the

afternoon, so that you have a chance to gather your thoughts and make a few notes about the places you have seen and whether or not you think the vendor would budge on the asking price.

7 Do not agree to see anything that is in the wrong place, is too expensive or does not have enough rooms. Don't, whatever you do, be swayed by the agent telling you things like, 'You'll be agreeably surprised – I think it's really worth you taking a look – properties like this don't come up very often – it's just come in today – I think you'll regret it if you don't – I just don't know when we'll have another one like it.' Keep an image of Arthur Daley firmly at the forefront of your mind, and tell the agent precisely your reasons for deciding that you are not going to view that property. If he persists in menacing you with threats – 'There won't be another like it' – tell him that's a risk you're prepared to take or 'That's a relief!', according to your mood.

8 Make sure you're not hungry – eat first!

We like it!

You are bound to find something you like sooner or later. Most people take about three months to find what they are looking for, although some find the ideal property in their first week of active searching while others may take two or three years. Statistics show, however, that three months is the average with four months being common; statistics also show, incidentally, with married couples that it is normally the woman who decides to move and the woman who gives the final 'Yes' or 'No'. So, don't feel discouraged and disheartened if nothing suitable turns up in the first month or two, or even longer.

If you are buying in England or Wales, you will make an offer *subject to survey and contract*, the subject of Chapter 3. In Scotland, your offer (which should be submitted through a solicitor in writing), once accepted, is legally binding. For this reason, you must have your lender's valuation and your own survey carried out *before* you make an offer. The search is carried out by the vendor before offers are received. Buyers in Scotland, then, happily, have no need to worry about a property already being under offer or the threat of being gazumped: they should, however, be prepared for a wasted survey fee.

Once you find something you like, don't let go. Tell the vendor you like it and that you will be in touch with the agent. If you are offered a cup of tea, accept, even if it means you are going to be late home. This provides you with an all-important opportunity of establishing a rapport and relationship with the vendor. Try to find out whether or not the vendor has already received an offer and, if so, what the position is. Has the offer been formally accepted? Has the other prospective buyer received an offer on his or her own property – in other words, is he or she in a position to proceed? Would the vendor be prepared to consider a higher offer, if he or she has not yet formally accepted an earlier one?

Already under offer

You may be surprised to learn that the vendor has already accepted a formal offer, and you may wonder why the agent has arranged for you to see the property at all. The reason why this very irritating situation occurs again and again is that estate agents often recommend that their client, in other words, the vendor, should continue to show the property in case the transaction breaks down. Some vendors, quite correctly, refuse to show the property once it is under offer. Others accept the agent's advice, however. The estate agent is required to pass on the details of *all* offers to his client. If a second prospective buyer makes an offer, in other words the vendor receives a second offer on the same property, the vendor may be tempted to withdraw from the first transaction and accept the second, higher offer – in other words, the first buyer is gazumped. Estate agents clearly have an incentive to encourage higher offers, as, if the vendor decides to accept, the agent's commission will be higher.

If the vendor indicates to you, as the second interested buyer, that he is prepared to gazump the first buyer, be very wary. He may do it to you as well – and you may have incurred legal and surveying fees before you find out. As a vendor, you can prevent a gazumping by declining to accept any offer for the first two weeks that the property is on sale. Then accept the best offer and stick with it. If you are yourself gazumped, as a buyer, there is nothing you can do. When you are house-hunting, therefore, it pays to ask the agent, before you view, whether or not the property is under offer. If it is, you may be wise to decline the opportunity to see it.

Considering making an offer

Once you have found something you like, get in touch with the agent as soon as possible, preferably the same day or the following morning to let them know that you are interested and that you are considering making an offer. Ask the agent what you think the buyer would accept. You would be wise at this point to consider a second viewing. Tell the agent that you intend to make an offer but that you would like to view again to make absolutely sure and to decide on the amount you are going to offer. You may think that there's no point to this second viewing if you already know that you'd like to make an offer, but in reality there are three good points.

First, you will notice things during a second viewing that you did not notice in the first. These may be attractive points, which confirm your initial response, or they may be drawbacks causing you to think again. A second viewing also gives you the opportunity to take another look at the surrounding area and the setting of the house. When you propose to spend as large a sum of money as this, it is wise to be certain.

The second point in favour of taking another look concerns how seriously the vendor and the agent are to take your offer. It is well known that vendors and agents are a little sceptical of the prospective purchaser who views once (perhaps for no more than 15–20 minutes) and makes an immediate offer. If, on the other hand, it can be seen that the purchaser has given the matter some thought, and has taken the trouble to view for a second time, the agent is likely to advise the vendor that this is a serious buyer and to recommend that the offer, if it is a reasonable one, should be accepted.

The third point concerns your relationship with the vendor. It is essential that you create between you an atmosphere of friendliness and trust. Both of you are about to embark on a business transaction that may continue for several months, with considerable problems and a large number of details to resolve. Although it is the task of the solicitors to do this, nothing will stand you in better stead than a good working relationship with your vendor – and indeed with your buyer, when you are the vendor. Delays and problems are almost inevitable in buying and selling property, and you will find it greatly to your advantage if you can resolve these quickly and amicably with your vendor or your buyer.

Your second viewing, then, gives you an opportunity of getting to know the vendor and deciding whether or not you think he or she is trustworthy and likely to act honourably (in other words, may refrain from gazumping or withdrawing the curtains that were originally included in the price, for example). You may also be able to establish why the vendor is moving – is it because of something about the property or the area that you don't yet know? Only instinct can guide you in these matters, but be alert. If you distrust the vendor on sight and suspect something fishy, you may well be wise not to enter a business transaction with them and to look for something else. Lastly, don't ever let a vendor know that you are absolutely desperate to buy the property, first, because you may be regarded as 'emotional' and therefore not a good person to do business with and, second, because it may encourage the vendor to put the price up. Equally, when you are yourself placed in the position of being the vendor, never admit you are desperate to sell, as your buyer may then make a low offer and you may be compelled to accept if you are indeed desperate. Be friendly and interested at all times, but never allow any anxiety you may be feeling to show!

The second viewing

You are now about to make your decision about whether or not to make a firm offer. This is the time to take a good overall look at the property, to confirm your positive feelings about it, to consider points of detail and to discuss a number of topics with the vendor. Before you go, take a good look at your list of features that you considered essential when you started your search for a new home. Does the property have all or most of the important ones? Is there something about the property that especially appeals to you? Have you had a good look around the area and checked on amenities, transport, schools and anything else that is of great importance to you? Can you afford it? Is it big enough? Will you be able to fit in your furniture? Think particularly about the large items, such as a double bed negotiating narrow stairs, a sofa or a piano. Do you consider the property safe? If you have children, is the road outside very busy? If you are a woman living alone, give some thought to the street lighting and to how secluded the entrance is.

Bear all these things in mind when you visit the property for the second time and, if necessary, keep a checklist in your pocket to which you can refer. During this visit, try, too, to be quite analytical about the condition of the property. Can you see obvious defects? Are the window frames rusted or rotten, depending on whether they are metal or wood? Can you see patches of damp? Is there a damp, musty smell? Can you see the condition of the gutters and downpipes (which together take the rainwater from the gutters to a soakaway at some distance from the property)? Will redecoration be an urgent priority? Take a look at the brickwork for cracks in the bricks and for the state of the mortar – does it look crumbly or are there bits missing, signifying a need for repointing? All these things may affect your final decision about the property and will certainly affect the amount you offer for it. If you notice anything that worries you, jot it down and remember to mention it to your surveyor so that he can either set your mind at rest or identify the problem and advise you how it may be resolved.

You need to be as alert as possible to the existence of any

serious defects. Structural problems reduce the value of a house very considerably, which means that your lender will not agree to advance you the amount that you need. If you go ahead, and apply for the loan and commission a survey without noticing such defects, it also means you may have wasted several hundred pounds on the valuation and full structural survey. So, look out for signs of general dilapidation; structural problems that could be indicated by a sagging roofline, cracks either in interior or exterior walls, or crumbling brickwork; signs of obvious cover-ups, such as newly decorated rooms, which may camouflage damp or condensation. Ask, too, if any work that has recently been carried out carries guarantees – as this gives you a clue about any past problems; you will also need these guarantees if you decide eventually to go ahead with the purchase. Any new house, in other words one that is less than ten years old, should have a National House Building Council certificate (NHBC certificate), which your lender will eventually wish to see. NHBC certificates constitute the builder's guarantee and last for ten years from the date of completion of the house. The last eight years of the guarantee covers only 'major defects.'

Nowhere is it more important than in Scotland to be certain that you like the property and that you have arranged appropriate finance. Here, you become legally bound to buy the property once your offer is accepted. If you are buying in Scotland, therefore, you should read all about the lender's valuation and your own survey, as well as specialist surveys (all discussed in the following chapter) *before* making an offer. You should arrange for insurance of the property once a written offer is accepted, and ensure that 'date of entry' (date of possession) coincides with what you have arranged with the buyer of your existing property.

Lastly, talk things over with the vendors and satisfy yourself it is their definite intention to sell. Ask them if they have found a property yet and, if so, how advanced they are with the purchase. If you sense that they are in a hurry to sell, ask yourself why and take this into account when you come to decide on the amount you are to offer. They may have to accept a low offer if their purchase is very advanced. On the other hand, your own property may be under offer, which means you are in a hurry to buy, yet you may be faced with a vendor who declares airily, 'Oh, we haven't really started looking yet . . .'. Some vendors are simply not serious about moving, while others appear to feel no sense of urgency. This can lead to you losing your prospective buyer, so beware becoming entangled with a desultory vendor. The second viewing, as well as giving you the opportunity to get to know the vendor, also allows you to ask about all sorts of things, such as local amenities and about such details as what they intend to leave in the way of curtains and carpets and so on. If you are genuinely interested in a property, the more detailed questions you ask the better, as this will help convince the vendor that your intentions are serious, as well as helping you work out a realistic budget.

The second viewing, then, is designed to help you make up your mind whether or not this is the property that you would like to be your next home. If you have any sense of doubt or disappointment at the time of the second viewing, think carefully before you go ahead. It may be wiser to continue the search. If you carry on looking, you are bound, in the end, to find something that you really like.

Most of us breathe a tremendous sigh of relief as we find the home we are looking for. However, the hunt is not quite over; although you have spotted your prey, you now have to secure it, first by making an acceptable offer and then by following through all the legal and financial stages of the transaction to the day of the move.

3

'Subject to survey and contract'

When you find the property that you think is the one for you, and you still think so after a second viewing and a discussion with the vendor, you are ready to make a formal offer either to the vendor's estate agent, or to the vendor direct in the case of a private sale. Before you make an offer, however, do reread the last few pages of the previous chapter, particularly the sections on *Considering making an offer* and *A second viewing*.

An offer is not legally binding (unless you are buying in Scotland), either upon you or upon the vendor, but it is nevertheless better to be sure. If you make an offer without being really sure, you may wish to withdraw, but you may by this time have already incurred legal and surveying fees. In addition, the estate agent will regard you as someone who does not know your own mind and will be reluctant to regard you as a serious buyer should you wish to make a subsequent offer on a different property with the same agent. A casual offer is also not fair to the vendor, who may make certain decisions and commitments on the strength of it. As a vendor yourself, it is up to you to ascertain whether or not your buyer is serious.

How much should I offer?

So, you have come to the point at which you would like to make an offer. Once you have decided, contact the vendor's agent or the vendor without delay – or someone may beat you to it. It is not wise to offer substantially less than the asking price, as this may be regarded as insulting and the offer not taken seriously.

What you offer for the property depends on the asking price, the method of selling and the terms in which the price is couched. In England and Wales, it is more or less accepted, unless the market is in a state of frenzy, that the buyer will be able to secure some sort of reduction. In Scotland, however, the prospective buyers note their offers on paper (the missives of sale), through a solicitor, and the person making the best offer is then accepted; this constitutes a firm contract. Buyers in Scotland cannot back out. Because of this, you must arrange your finance and a survey of the property *in advance of* making an offer.

In England and Wales, the buyer may often obtain a reduction at this initial stage and may obtain a further reduction should the survey prove unfavourable. If the property is being auctioned, you will need to have a survey carried out before the auction, as you will then be legally bound to buy the house. Lastly, the terms in which the price is couched give you a clue about the figure expected:

'O.I.R.O. (or 'Offers in the region of') £xx,xxx' = You can probably get some reduction

'Offers in excess of £xx,xxx' = You need to offer more than the stated price

'Tenders invited over £xx,xxx' = Each prospective buyer makes an offer and the highest wins

The price itself also sometimes offers clues. For example, £57,950 would have to be read as £58,000 in a frenzied market when properties are snapped up within a week of being put on sale; however, it could also be read as £57,500 (the extra £450 having been asked as a means of ensuring offers of £57,500). If the price asked is £57,500, an offer of £57,000 may be accepted. £102,000, in the same way, can be read as £100,000 in all but the most frenzied times. The higher the price, the more difficult it is to assess what you need to offer to secure the property. One way round this is to sound out the vendor, rather than the agent: 'Would you take a little less?' or, 'May I ask what your lowest figure would be – it's just slightly out of our range but we *are* interested'. It also may help you to try and identify the vendors' reasons for moving and whether or not they have found a new home. If they have to move, and they have also found something that they like, you may assume that they will accept a lower offer provided that they can see it is a serious one and that you can go ahead without delay.

It is worth asking the vendor's agent what he thinks the vendors would accept. Remember that the agent is acting for the vendors and he will, therefore, know exactly how easy or how difficult the property in question is to sell and in how much of a hurry the vendor is. It is, furthermore, in the agent's interest to get the property sold as quickly as possible so that he receives his commission sooner rather than later. For this reason, the agent may be willing to establish your top figure and then recommend it to his client, even though it may be lower than what the vendor had hoped for. The agent may even press the vendor to accept a figure that is really not in the vendor's best interests, just for a quick sale. He may then continue to show the property and this may result in the vendor receiving a higher offer, who will then be sorely tempted to accept it and gazump you.

How much you offer, then, is quite crucial to the outcome of the transaction.

Making the offer

Simply telephone the agent and tell him how much you would like to offer for the property and that your offer is *subject to survey and contract*. The agent will get back to you within 24 hours to let you know if the vendor has accepted. If he has, the agent will ask you for the name and address of your solicitor and may also ask you for a deposit of about £100 or so. You will see, if you look back to the start of Chapter 1, that this deposit is not obligatory, but it may nevertheless be worth your while paying it. If you pay a deposit, be sure to obtain a receipt on the agent's letterhead. The receipt should be signed and dated.

You should now instruct your solicitor that you wish to go ahead with the purchase of the property, confirm the price (subject to survey and contract), give the name of the vendor and the address of the property, together with the name and telephone number of the agent. It is well worth while making a telephone call to the vendor with the words: 'I'm delighted that you have accepted our offer. I hope everything goes smoothly. Do ring me if there are problems or delays.' And make sure that they have your telephone number. Although estate agents are meant to see the sale through, they often do not, particularly at busy periods and this sometimes results in losing the property altogether. It is wise, therefore, for buyer and vendor to keep in touch, at least weekly, in order to monitor progress.

The next steps

It is most important, if you are also selling a property, that you keep tabs on your sale. Your agent, if you are using one, may or may not ask your buyer for a deposit: ask your agent if he has asked your buyer for a deposit and, if so, whether it has been paid. You will have given your buyer the name and address of your solicitor, so that your buyer's solicitors can start the legal processes. Check within a week or two of receiving an offer on your property that your solicitor has heard from your buyer's solicitors. If your buyer seems a bit slow, get on to your estate agent and ask him to find out what is happening.

Once your offer has been accepted on the property you wish to buy, the next steps are for the two sets of solicitors to make contact, the local search to be initiated (by your solicitor), the vendor's solicitor to obtain deeds from the existing lender on the property, and to send a draft contract with a copy of the deeds to your solicitor. Your solicitor will then raise the pre-contract enquiries based on these documents. You should alert your lender (the building society or bank) and fill in your mortgage application form. The lender will then arrange for their valuation survey to be carried out. You may be asked at this point if you wish to 'top-up' the fee for the valuation survey so that the surveyor carries out a full structural survey for you at the same time that he does the valuation for the lender. Opinion is divided on the wisdom of this.

Two surveys in one

It is normally cheaper to top-up the lender's valuation fee and have your full structural survey done by the same person at the same time. However, how efficient a practice this is is debatable.

Banks often nominate local estate agents to carry out their valuation, rather than a local surveyor who will have more experience of surveying and, perhaps, more detailed knowledge of the housing stock in the area and local conditions (such as a river that may flood, for example). The second factor against having two surveys performed in one is that some people consider it preferable to see how the property comes out in the not very expensive valuation survey before they commit themselves to a full structural. The third point to be made is that, simply, one pair of eyes can never be as efficient as two.

If you are pressed both for time and for money, however, there is something to be said for having both surveys done at the same time. A final point to bear in mind is that although the lender will nominate the surveyor to carry out the valuation, you may if you wish ask them to use the surveyor of your choice. They will probably agree, provided that your surveyor is qualified, with the initials FRICS or ARICS after his name.

If you have a special reason for being unwilling for the lender to use a particular agent/valuer, inform the lender of this. For example, we found a house that we liked in the summer of 1987 through a large chain of estate agents. We discovered from the vendor that the local estate agent (with whom we were in regular contact) had had the house on its books for at least two months but, for some reason, its particulars had not been sent to us. The vendor also told us that the local agent was annoyed at not having been able to sell the house. The bank decided to nominate this local agent to carry out their valuation! I could see that this was not an awfully good idea and arranged, therefore, with the lender for a different, local, full-time surveyor to carry out both the valuation and the full structural survey at the same time.

It is worth bearing in mind that the branch managers of building societies and banks often have their favourite valuers, but 'favourite' does not necessarily mean 'best'. 'Favourite' may mean that they have a business or social association with them which it is to their advantage to further. While you mull over the pros and cons of two surveys in one, look back to Chapter 1 for guidance about the fees you will be charged.

Keeping in touch

The most important thing you can do to help the transaction along is to keep in touch regularly with the parties concerned: the vendor, the vendor's agent, your solicitor and the lender. Deal with any paperwork promptly and check with your solicitor that the local search has been initiated and with the vendor that the lender's valuer has arranged a date for the survey. Ask the vendor to let you know if the lender's valuation has not been carried out within a reasonable time of when you informed them of your intention to buy the property (say, three weeks). As for the local search – which sometimes delays the entire transaction for a month or more – ask your solicitor how long the local council normally takes. If he heaves a sigh, tell him that you are prepared to pay for a private search should timing become crucial.

If you are also selling a property, it is essential that you keep in regular contact with your buyer. If things go quiet, do not assume that everything is going smoothly: it could mean that your buyer is having second thoughts. The sale of your property probably has to dovetail with the purchase of your new home, in order to avoid an expensive bridging loan, so, without appearing over-anxious, do what you can to make sure that things are moving along.

What happens next

The sequence of events tends to vary on individual transactions in accordance with how efficient each organization is. The things you need to keep tabs on are:

- the local search
- the lender's valuation
- your own survey and any specialist surveys
- the type of mortgage you select
- the amount the lender is prepared to offer, which depends on the outcome of their valuation

- responses to pre-contract enquiries and draft contract, both of which you will receive from your solicitor
- legal processes, such as establishing proof of title and checking the terms of the lease, all of which will be carried out by your solicitor
- renegotiating the price of the property as a consequence of one of the points above: how much the lender thinks the property is worth, how many defects your own surveyor discovers, the amount your lender is prepared to offer, significant drawbacks revealed by the preliminary pre-contract enquiries
- buildings insurance on the property you intend to buy, which should run from the date of exchange of contracts (which will be a few weeks before you move in), because once contracts have been exchanged, you are legally bound to buy the house even if it burns to the ground before you set foot in it (the lender often offers to arrange the building insurance as it is clearly in their interest that the property is adequately covered)
- the sale of your existing home.

The local search

This enquiry, made by your solicitor of the council in whose area the property is located, is intended to reveal planning restrictions or enforcement notices and anything else that may adversely affect the property. It is important that the solicitor asks the council of the existence of any regulation or condition that may affect the property *or the surrounding area*. You need to know, for example, if a new road is planned or being discussed, if you are below a flight path, if the area is regularly flooded and if anything exists that has already caused complaints from local residents, such as low flying aircraft or night flights.

Your solicitor will probably point out to you that this search can only give you the facts as they existed at the time of the enquiry and also that only definitive proposals and applications will be disclosed. If, for example, planning permission is granted on what you regarded as the rolling hills in the distance beyond your garden a couple of months after the search, the council cannot be held responsible. It is up to you to take into account such possibilities and enquire of the council the designation of such land – is it agricultural or building land?

The lender's valuation

You will recall from Chapter 1 that you should not base your decision on whether or not to buy upon this valuation survey. This survey is intended only to confirm to the lender that the property is worth roughly the asking price. It is not intended to reveal any serious defects (which could, in fact, reduce the value of the property). All the lender wants to know is can he re-sell the property for the asking price in the event of you being unable to meet the mortgage repayments. Most lenders now make it clear to their clients that they must not rely on such valuations.

The valuation may put the value of the house lower than the amount you have offered for it. This means that the lender may not offer as much as you had hoped. Before you can decide what to do about this, you will have to take into account the information you receive in your own survey, the type of mortgage you have chosen and your overall budget.

Your own survey

You can have a full structural survey as noted in Chapter 1 or, for two-thirds of the cost, an RICS Housebuyer's or Flatbuyer's Report which tells you what you need to know and is therefore regarded as a bargain.

There are exceedingly few houses that are perfect in every respect of structure, fabric and internal and external decoration, but it is your surveyor's duty to point out any defects or deficiencies, irrespective of how serious or how minor they may be. Your surveyor's lengthy report could, therefore, include comments on the condition of the roof (which could be serious) and the condition of the door handles (which would be unlikely to affect in any way your decision to buy the property). Surveyors, in common with doctors and solicitors, are under considerable pressure not to overlook any fine point that could, in the eyes of the client, have some significant bearing on any action that the client then took. These two factors combine to compel any surveyor to produce a report, of some 15 or so typed pages, which typically makes depressing reading. Even a well-built, good quality, well-maintained house can appear to be slightly substandard when viewed through the eyes of a surveyor. If you are considering a property which does need attention, and even to a non-professional eye has problems, you may safely assume that the surveyor's report will be quite alarming. In view of all this, you have to know how to interpret such reports.

First, look at the *degree* of any problem and, secondly, work out in which *category* or *trade* it falls into, with a view to obtaining estimates from the relevant contractor.

As far as *degree* is concerned, you should regard any of the following as serious:

- 'needs immediate attention'
- 'constitutes a major/serious defect'
- 'is unsafe'
- 'allows the penetration of rainwater'
- 'possibility of structural weakness, dry rot, wet rot (damp)'
- 'fire hazard'.

Now look at the categories:

1 Structural/severe cracks in brickwork/possibility of subsidence/sinking. Any such comment has serious implications and you should delay your decision to purchase until you have commissioned and received a report from a structural engineer. The report in many cases reassures the prospective buyer with the advice: 'There are signs of gradual movement, but this is nothing more than would be expected.' If there is a genuine and severe structural problem, however, you would be wise not to take on the property, unless you are able to budget for the building work to be done. Your lender will, in addition, refuse to offer the maximum figure on such a property.

2 Roof – anything to do with the roof can be budgeted for after you have had a roofing contractor look at the problem.

3 Dry rot, damp, condensation, woodworm or other infestation – can be examined by a specialist firm and quotations obtained for the work.

4 Rainwater goods – this will refer to the gutters and downpipes, the efficient functioning of which are important in order to prevent the penetration of rain, and consequent dampness of the house. If these are defective, you will need either a builder or a good plumber and a budget of several hundred pounds.

5 Flaking plaster, spongy floors, a musty smell and moist skirting all points to some sort of rot – either wet or dry – and should be investigated by a specialist firm. Dry rot is notoriously difficult to arrest and expensive and disruptive to treat. Damp rot is a less serious problem than dry rot, but it can, nevertheless, prove very expensive and disruptive to remedy.

6 External treatment and decoration of the property. If this is in a very poor state, rain may penetrate and cause dampness and associated deterioration of the fabric of the property. You need to know, therefore, that external window frames are neither flaking, rusted nor rotten and that the external doors are in good condition and fit their frame properly. If not, this is something you will, with the help of a builder, have to budget for.

7 Services or systems, which include electrical, plumbing and drainage. All these systems deteriorate with age, so you may assume that work will need to be done if any of them are more than 20 years old. Specialist surveys can be carried out on the electrical, plumbing and drainage systems. The reports will identify what needs doing and the likely costs. You should approach a good firm of electricians (through personal recommendation) or your local electricity board; a good firm of general builders or plumbing contractors; a specialist drains contractor, either through personal recommendation or through a good general builder. A surveyor can only comment on what he believes to be the age and condition of these systems; he will not be able to determine whether or not they function safely and efficiently, so specialist reports are to be recommended.

8 Internal decoration. This is not crucial and you can in any case determine the state of the decoration for yourself. All properties need redecorating every few years, so don't be depressed if the surveyor indicates that the decoration is 'in need of renewal', 'a bit tired', 'shoddily done' or 'in a generally poor state'. The only words you need to worry about are 'bulging', 'flaking', 'peeling', 'blistering', any one of which could indicate wet or dry rot.

9 Floor coverings. Surveyors are not normally allowed by the vendor to remove fitted carpets or lino, for obvious reasons. This means that they may be unable to determine the condition of the flooring and the joists, and would, therefore, be unable to identify rising damp, for example. If, therefore, the surveyor describes any *other* sign of dampness or rot (such as at floor level or around the skirtings), you would be well advised to ask the vendor to allow a specialist company to make a thorough inspection and agree that you will pay for a carpet contractor to refit the carpets afterwards. If the vendor refuses, you should ask yourself why; and, if you decide to go ahead without this important inspection, you would be wise to budget for remedial work to be done by a specialist company and allow, of course, for the associated disruption.

10 Odds and ends. Surveyors typically comment on door handles and loo roll holders if they are in a less than perfect condition – but you can ignore such minor problems, as, in the context of a very large investment of money, they are virtually irrelevant. You should always take these comments in their entire context, however. If, for example, the surveyor writes that the door handle is wobbly, the door doesn't appear to fit the frame and the frame has shifted, then you should ask why, in his opinion, is this so. Does he suspect a structural fault, for example? Another example of an apparently innocent comment is offered by the surveyor who wrote 'The shower tiles need a bit of tidying up'. In this true example, the floor tiles surrounding the shower were cracked, indicating that movement had taken place. The fact that they were cracked should have indicated to the surveyor that they were no longer waterproof. When these tiles were removed, prior to being replaced, it was discovered that the wooden floor beneath was completely rotten and some of the joists were also wet. Had this situation been allowed to continue – in other words, had the new owner disregarded the advice about 'tidying up the shower tiles' – the ceiling in the room below (the kitchen) would eventually have come down. This cautionary tale does not reflect well upon the surveyor concerned, but, more important, it is intended to encourage you to ask your surveyor searching questions when you receive his report.

Getting advice about a mortgage

There are a number of different sources of advice about obtaining a mortgage, the type of mortgage and the amount. These include:

1 Your bank manager. His advice will be free but he will hope to sell you a mortgage through his bank's home loans department. The bank will benefit further by selling you an endowment mortgage (see p. 65) as the insurance company issuing the endowment policy will pay a commission.

2 The home loans department of your bank or any other bank. Again, the advice is free, but banks' home loans departments exist for the sole purpose of making money by lending money to others, such as you, in return for the payment of interest.

3 Any building society. Again, the advice is free, but, in common with banks' home loans departments, their business is to sell mortgages.

4 A mortgage or insurance broker. Once again, the advice is free – but, once again, brokers survive by selling mortgages and insurance packages, including endowment policies. They receive commission from the organization that arranges the mortgage and from the insurance company that arranges any related policy, such as endowment or pension.

5 If you have an accountant, he or she should be able to offer you objective and independent advice and to explain to you which is the best type of mortgage for you, taking into

account your individual circumstances. This professional, as opposed to commercial, advice is chargeable to you.

6 Solicitors vary in the extent to which they are prepared to offer professional advice about finance. Some solicitors handle their clients' affairs for them almost completely, while others prefer to point you in the direction of the right sort of commercial organization. They will, in all probability, recommend you to approach a number of organizations and urge you to obtain several mortgage proposals in order to make a comparison. Your solicitor may charge you for such advice.

Whichever route you choose, it is always best to consult either someone you already know, and have had dealings with, or someone for whom you have a personal recommendation from someone whose opinion you respect. Don't be tempted to respond to advertisements which claim: 'You want a mortgage – that's easy . . .' and don't allow yourself to be talked into borrowing more than you can afford (the monthly repayment figure should not exceed, ideally, more than one-third of your net monthly income). Be careful to check the interest rate, as well, by consulting a daily newspaper or by telephoning your local branch of any bank.

Mortgage brokers sometimes succeed in obtaining mortgages for people whose own efforts have failed. This is sometimes managed by the broker arranging the loan at a higher interest rate, and may not, therefore, be in your best interests. For example, my sister was once offered a 14.5 per cent mortgage on a 'difficult' property when the current rate was 10.5 per cent. In cases of properties that could be difficult to sell, mortgagors typically either refuse to offer a mortgage or seek to cover any potential risk by offering a mortgage on punitive terms. If a lender views a property as a high risk, perhaps you should, too, and look around for something else.

Which type of mortgage?

Building societies and banks offer a number of different types of mortgage, usually at different repayment rates and with different conditions attached to them. For this reason it is worth obtaining 'illustrations' (the term for a sheet of figures outlining the amount of loan and the repayments, both gross and net) from at least one bank and one building society, if not more.

When you receive all the illustrations, you should check that you compare like with like – in other words, beware of confusing gross with net when you look at the repayment figures. 'Gross' means before tax relief; 'net' means the figure you will pay net of tax, in other words, after tax relief has been applied. You should also enquire, when you look at net figures, what rate of tax has been assumed in order to make sure that it is the same rate as your top rate. If, for example, you pay tax at the higher rate of 40 per cent, rather than at the basic rate (currently 25 per cent), you will receive tax relief at 40 per cent. Check, too, that the mortgage term is the same. Although it is usually 25 years, it can be 20 or 30 years. Most mortgages have to be repaid in full by retirement age, so the mortgage term can in fact vary from 10 to 35 years.

The three main categories of mortgage are repayment, endowment and pension. The various types include:

- repayment mortgages (also referred to as capital repayment mortgages), including low-start mortgages
- endowment mortgages
- low cost endowment mortgages
- with-profits endowment mortgages
- pension mortgages
- unit-linked mortgages
- fixed rate mortgages
- interest-only mortgages

A repayment mortgage involves the monthly repayment of some of the capital (the amount of loan) and some of the interest upon the loan. Because the capital amount decreases throughout the term of the mortgage (usually 25 years) the amount of interest also decreases. This means that the monthly repayments represent an *increasing* amount of capital and a *decreasing* amount of interest. Tax relief is applied only to the interest payment and this means that tax relief decreases over the years. This can have the net effect over the mortgage term of a gradual increase in the annual repayments. Those people with salaries that are expected to *increase* over the years, rather than remain static or decrease, and who also may be paying substantial tax, will not find this type of mortgage 'tax-efficient' as their tax relief goes down just when they need it to go up, and thus their mortgage is costing them more than it need.

Low start capital repayment mortgages may offer an attractive option for young first-time buyers. These work on the principle of capital repayment, in which the monthly repayment comprises some capital and some interest. However, with the low start variation, the capital element of the repayment is 'rolled over' for the first five or ten years, so that in Year One, interest only and no capital are repaid, in Year Two, interest plus a small amount of capital (say, £500) is repaid, in Year Three interest plus, say, £1000 of capital is repaid, and so on. Clearly, low start must mean 'high later on' because the capital is not reduced at all in the early years of the mortgage term and thus increases the amount of interest payable. Rather than level monthly repayments, payments are calculated so that they are lower for the first five or ten years of the mortgage and then gradually rise for the remainder of the term.

If you are interested in this sort of mortgage, it is worth bearing in mind that it would be unwise, financially, to consider moving in the first few years of the mortgage term as it would be difficult to recoup your costs. As one home loans expert has put it, 'You're going nowhere in the first two or three years' towards repaying the loan.

Young first-time buyers are recommended to compare low start capital repayment mortgages with low cost endowment mortgages (see below) to determine which suit their personal circumstances the best. If the low cost endowment mortgage repayment (which comprises an interest payment *plus* an endowment policy premium) amounts to not too much more than the low start capital repayment figure, and the endowment is guaranteed (rather than 'expected') to cover the loan at the end of the term, it is probably safe to say that the endowment is the better bet.

People whose earnings are expected to rise in future years may do better with one of the types of *endowment mortgages* (provided that interest rates are not high), in which none of the loan is repaid until the end of the term and the monthly repayments consist of (1) interest upon the loan (but no capital) and (2) a monthly premium in respect of an endowment (life assurance) policy. Endowment mortgages require the mortgagee to take out a life assurance policy for the amount of the loan. This is set to mature at the end of the mortgage term (usually 25 years) and is then used to pay off the loan. When interest rates are comparatively low, and particularly in the case of high earners, endowment mortgages are undoubtedly attractive, since tax relief is maximized. With repayment mortgages, the amount of interest, and therefore the amount of tax relief, decreases throughout the term.

Low cost endowment mortgages are particularly helpful for the young, first-time buyer whose salary is likely to rise as they are tax-efficient and are cheaper than a full endowment mortgage. The endowment amount is less than for a full endowment and it may not be *guaranteed* to be sufficient to repay the mortgage at term.

With-profits endowment mortgages involve paying higher monthly repayments with the aim of not only repaying the interest and the premium for the life cover but also of receiving a tax-free lump sum at the end of the term. This is simply a tax-efficient method of saving money for one's retirement at the same time as buying a home.

The most important question to ask when considering an endowment mortgage is 'How flexible is it?'. What happens if you want to move home again, perhaps five, perhaps ten years, into the term of the mortgage? Can the endowment be 'topped-up' in the event of buying a more expensive property?

If you elect for a capital repayment mortgage, you will

probably be asked to take out a mortgage protection policy so that repayment of the mortgage is guaranteed in the event of your death before term. In the case of a married couple, who may have taken both salaries into account in determining the amount of the mortgage, this means that the mortgage is cleared in the event of death of either spouse before term so that the surviving spouse is not faced with repaying the mortgage from one salary.

This sort of policy is unnecessary in the case of endowment mortgages as the endowment policy itself extends life assurance cover. The policy either clears the mortgage at term or, in the event of the death of a mortgagee, before term. This means that the surviving spouse of a married couple, again, is relieved of the burden of repaying the mortgage on a single salary.

Pension mortgages have tended to be less flexible than repayment or endowment mortgages, but this is now less of a problem since the introduction of portable pension plans. It used to be the case that an employee had to join the company pension scheme, which meant that each time an employee changed jobs, his pension scheme would be terminated and another one started. It is now possible for employees to carry their personal pension scheme from one firm to another, so that pension mortgages now look more attractive. They are highly tax efficient, but it must be pointed out that you need to set the pension amount due on retirement at a sufficiently high level to accommodate both the repayment of the mortgage loan *and* adequate pension arrangements for life. If you are interested in this type of mortgage, be sure to ask how they differ from the other two categories in terms of flexibility, for the rules tend to vary from one lender to another.

Monthly repayments comprise three payments: an interest-only payment on the amount of loan; premiums on a pension policy; and premiums on a term life insurance policy to cover your death before retirement.

Unit-linked mortgages are a type of endowment mortgage with the important difference that their 'performance' depends on how well the stock market is doing. An endowment mortgage is geared to make sure that you receive adequate funds to repay the mortgage loan at term, and, as such, the investments made on your behalf are 'safe'. Unit-linked loans are more closely geared to the fluctuations of the stock market and, therefore, may produce a much higher sum than the loan amount at term, or a lower sum – in which case you would have to find the difference.

Fixed rate mortgages, which are not easy to find, are those in which the interest rate is fixed for some years at a time, say five, and then renegotiated. These are attractive principally for peace of mind, since your mortgage repayments cannot increase during the fixed term even if the Chancellor of the Exchequer should decide to increase interest rates five times in a year. Clearly, the figure at which the interest rate is fixed is crucial.

Interest-only mortgages are designed for the elderly. In common with endowment mortgages, none of the loan is repaid through the monthly repayments. There is no need for endowment or other life cover, however. The loan is repaid on the death of the mortgagee or of both mortgagees in the case of a couple. For example, if a married couple of retirement age buy a £100,000 house, they can raise a £30,000 mortgage and repay each month the interest upon the £30,000. The loan is repaid on the death of both parties.

It must be stressed that the best type of mortgage for you depends on a number of factors and this is why it is recommended that you look into the matter fully and obtain various illustrations for the different types. The factors include your age, current salary and salary expectations, tax rate, the prevailing interest rate, the amount of loan required and the period for which it is required. First time buyers should look at low start capital repayment mortgages or low cost endowment mortgages.

The amount of mortgage

Building societies and banks differ on the amount that they are prepared to lend to any individual or any married couple and it is therefore advisable to approach more than one potential lender. Some lenders will offer 2½–3 times your salary (or your net profit if self-employed). In the case of married couples, some will offer

2½–3 times the salary of the higher earner and add the amount of the salary of the lower earner. To demonstrate this, if you earn £10,000 a year, you may be able to borrow as much as £30,000; if you earn £16,000, you may be able to borrow as much as £48,000. If your partner earns £20,000 and you earn £10,000, you may be able to borrow as much as £70,000. Some lenders will offer 2–2¼ times the amount of a couple's joint income. There is a considerable variation in these rules of thumb, however, so be sure to get several illustrations from several sources before you make a decision.

Most lenders will not normally include overtime or commission payments as part of your salary figure; they look at your basic salary. You will have to furnish proof of your salary, either in the form of your last three payslips if you are on PAYE, or, if you are self-employed, you will have to provide the lender with three years' audited figures (prepared by an accountant).

Finally, building societies and banks are usually reluctant to lend more than 90 per cent of the value of the property, the value having been set by their valuer, rather than the vendor's asking price. If you are looking at a £100,000 property, therefore, the lender will probably not want to lend more than £90,000 and will only lend that if your salary justifies it – £30,000 in other words. It is possible to obtain 95 per cent and 100 per cent mortgages, particularly in the case of first-time buyers, but these are often payable at higher rates in order to justify the lender's increased risk. Lenders tend to feel that you should have saved something towards the cost of the property, or alternatively have some collateral, or security, to offer. Evidence shows that those who are able to put something towards the cost of the property have a better record in keeping up with mortgage repayments and a better record in maintaining the property.

Pre-contract enquiries

At the same time as you are arranging your mortgage and deliberating over the bank and building society illustrations, you will probably receive your solicitor's Report on the property, including the responses to the pre-contract enquiries, which will have been sent by your vendor's solicitor to your solicitor. If you also have a property to sell, you, as the vendor, will be required to respond to a long list of questions in the same way. These preliminary enquiries are intended to reveal any problems with the purchase of the property and form the basis of the contract to buy.

One of the most important points concerns the status of the property, in other words, whether it is leasehold or freehold. Buying or selling a leasehold property is often more complicated than buying or selling a freehold, and you are therefore recommended to discuss the clauses of a lease that you intend to buy in detail with your solicitor (see *Freehold or leasehold?* in Chapter 2). Remember that when you buy a property on a leasehold basis, you are buying, in fact, a lease on it, rather than the property itself. It is essential, therefore, to understand fully the terms of the lease and to be confident that what you are buying will, in the future, when you may wish to sell it, prove saleable.

Pre-contract enquiries cover a large number of points, which may include:

1 The location of the title deeds of the property.
2 Ownership of the boundaries (such as fences and walls).
3 Disputes with neighbours.
4 Legal notices served by the local authority.
5 Connections to mains drainage, water, gas, electricity, telephone.
6 Whether or not anyone other than the vendor has any claim upon the property being sold.
7 Any breach of any covenant relating to the property.
8 The construction of the property; condition of the wiring; woodworm and damp treatment; the condition of the roof; insulation; any relevant guarantees for work carried out.
9 The existence of additions, extensions, or structural alterations, and associated planning permissions.
10 Authorized planning use for the property.

11 Fire regulations.
12 Ownership of roads, passageways and alleys abutting the property.
13 Ownership and maintenance of side alleys.
14 Compulsory purchase orders, tree preservation orders, clearance schemes, road construction or widening near the property, local flooding, structural or other defects to the property, damp, dry rot or woodworm infestation, other latent defects, details of policy of insurance presently effected and any special conditions applied to the policy which could affect the cover extended.
15 Structures in the garden, building regulation consents, susceptibility of garden to flooding.
16 Does the property conform to the Clean Air Act 1956?
17 Details of fittings and fixtures: what is to be included in the purchase price and what is to be removed.
18 The existence of easements (which might grant others a legal access to your property, such as the existence of a public right of way).
19 Details of central heating.
20 Any unusual outgoings.
21 Any planning proposals affecting neighbouring land or premises.
22 Clearance of the property and garden, other than agreed fixtures and fittings, by the vendor.
23 Timing of exchange of contracts and completion.
24 Parking arrangements.
25 Reduction of the 10 per cent deposit, normally paid on exchange of contracts.
26 Details of the telephone apparatus and line. Whether the vendors intend to take the telephone itself or the number with them.
27 In the case of leasehold, details of service charges and other outgoings, including insurance premiums.

As you see, the pre-contract enquiries require the vendor to answer questions on a large number of topics and for the buyer's solicitor to consider each response carefully and advise you, as his client, on the implications. These questions are sometimes answered with meaningless phrases such as 'Not to our knowledge' or 'Not as far as we are aware', or 'To be advised'. Make sure that you receive satisfactory responses to all the questions your solicitor has put to the vendor's solicitor; some of them could have important implications. When you are selling your own property, as the vendor, try to answer the questions as fully and informatively as possible. A little extra effort at this stage may save valuable time later. If any of the questions worry you, or you are uncertain how to respond, discuss the matter with your solicitor.

Renegotiating the price

The lender's valuation has been done, your own survey has been carried out, you have had discussions and received quotations from a number of building societies or banks and you are alerted, through the pre-contract enquiries, to any potential problems with the property. You are now in a position, therefore, to sit back and think over all the information you have received and make an informed decision about the wisdom of buying the property in question at the price you offered. Are you happy about going ahead and, if so, should you consider negotiating a reduction in the figure you originally offered? Your offer was made *subject to survey and contract*; and this is the time to assess whether the offer is reasonable in the light of the knowledge you now have or whether the offer should be revised.

If the lender's valuation survey or your own survey (or any of your specialist surveys) have revealed potentially serious and expensive problems with the property, you would be wise to renegotiate the offer price, either with the vendor's estate agent or the vendor directly; alternatively, your solicitor may be willing to do it for you. Success will depend on these factors:

- how keen are the vendors to sell?
- how crucial is the asking price to their budget?
- how likely are they to be able to find an alternative buyer?
- how many, if any, of the defects were apparent to you (either

71

because the vendor told you of them or because no one with eyes could possibly have missed them)?

- how skilled and how determined are you in financial negotiation?

If you know, for example, that the vendors are keen to sell and are well advanced with their new purchase, that the market is a bit slow and that none of the defects were apparent, you may have a good chance provided that you make a convincing case. If, on the other hand, only some of the factors weigh in your favour, you will have to choose between being ruthless, saying, 'We're not prepared to buy the property without a substantial reduction in view of these defects', and being somewhat less hard-headed in order not to risk losing the property altogether. If, of course, the defects combine to make the property simply too expensive, then you have no alternative but to put your case and press for a reduction. If you fail, you will have to let the property go – but it may be at this point that the vendor gives in, realizing that you are indeed serious, and offers a decent reduction, allowing you to go ahead.

Clearly, you have to take chances in this situation if you are to succeed; if you push too hard, however, you may lose out. This is why I suggested at the start of the book that buying and selling property is best regarded as a business matter. If you fall in love with a property, it will be difficult for you to distinguish what makes good financial sense and what doesn't. If the defects add up to £10,000, for example, you are in effect throwing away that amount of money by buying a property for £10,000 more than it should cost.

The sale of your existing home

Having read this chapter you will appreciate the many things that your buyer, if you are also selling a property, is doing in order to secure the purchase of your existing property. Do keep in touch with your buyer in order to reassure yourself that everything is moving along. The checks you can make include:

1 Checking with your solicitor that your buyer's solicitors have contacted him.

2 Asking your solicitor if he or she expects a delay in your buyer receiving the local search; and, if so, asking your buyer to consider making a private search should this hold up the transaction.

3 Noting the date on which the offer was made so that if you have not been informed of the date on which the valuer is to carry out the survey for your buyer's lender within two or three weeks, you can alert your buyer/estate agent/solicitor.

4 Asking your buyer if they intend to have a full survey and, if so, when is it likely to be done.

5 Getting your estate agent to check your buyer has arranged for a mortgage, unless he or she happens to be a cash buyer.

6 Dealing promptly with the pre-contract questionnaire, so that your solicitor may send your responses to your buyer's solicitor. If it does not arrive within, say, two weeks of your receiving the offer, talk to your solicitor about it.

7 Dealing with any queries your buyer may raise in a friendly and informative manner.

Don't be so efficient and assertive that you frighten off your buyer: I am not suggesting you do all the things listed above, merely some of them. The worst that can happen is that your buyer is not serious, or cannot raise the finance, and you don't realize this until too late when you are at risk of losing the property you want to buy.

Smoothing things over

It is vital that you maintain a friendly relationship with both your vendor, and your buyer, too, if you happen to be selling at the same time, so that if problems, including having to renegotiate the price, occur, you can resolve them in as efficient and amicable a manner as possible. Equally, all sorts of delays and mishaps beset both vendors and purchasers, and, although they are frequently not of their own making, it is in the interests of both parties to see that they are sorted out. Typical problems are the subject of the following chapter.

4

Fighting disaster

All sorts of slips and delays combine to make the few weeks before exchange of contracts quite nerve-wracking for many of us. The sorts of thing discussed in this chapter tend to happen only in England and Wales – in Scotland your offer, once accepted, is legally binding: it is not subject to survey and contract and you therefore cannot be gazumped.

The first rule is communication: keep in regular contact with your vendor, your buyer if you are also selling, and your solicitor. Make sure that you speak to each once a week, unless it is clearly unnecessary. Deal with any forms and paperwork as soon as you receive them and use first-class post.

You will need to think about what fittings and fixtures you hope to buy from the vendor, and agree a price for each item. If you are also selling a property, think about the fittings and fixtures you intend to offer your buyer. You can be certain of what you would like to buy from your vendor only when you have established what you are selling to your buyer and what you will be taking with you. If you are buying at just over £30,000 and carpets or curtains were included in the asking price for your new home, be sure that your solicitor appreciates this as he can then attach a figure to them, deduct it from the offer figure and thus save you stamp duty (see page 10).

Fittings and fixtures may not seem very important at this stage, but they can, in fact, cause delays at the exchange of contract stage and disputes can arise through neither vendor nor buyer giving some thought to what may seem like details.

Disasters just before exchange of contracts fall into two categories: those which threaten your prospective purchase and those which threaten your sale. Each hinges upon the other, unfortunately, in that if you lose the property you want to buy, you may have to let your buyer go while you search for another property, and if you lose your buyer you may not be able to get a second buyer quickly enough to catch up with your own purchase. The only way out of this would be to take an expensive bridging loan. By now you will have incurred both legal and surveying fees, and so, provided that you are sure you want to buy the property you are in the process of acquiring, it is essential to do what you can to make sure that both transactions go through smoothly and on time.

In the same way as you may have both a vendor and a buyer, so may the other parties. This means that there may be a chain of vendors and buyers, each dependent upon the next for the successful outcome of their own transaction. For example, you may have Mr van Hegarty, a first-time buyer at the bottom of the chain. Being a first-time buyer, it may take him longer to obtain a mortgage and he probably won't know the ropes. He is buying from two freelances, Mr McGrath and Ms Callagher, both of whom must have accountants prepare three years of audited figures before they can obtain their mortgage. They are buying from two lecturers, Mr and Mrs Lashmar. They are buying from Mr and Ms Thorpe, who in turn are buying from Dr and Mrs Cutting. The Cuttings intend to buy from the Hardings, who, in turn, are buying a new house from a builder, who has imposed a deadline for the exchange of contracts. There the chain stops. So, there are twelve transactions, involving seven firms of solicitors and their clients, in this chain.

Complex chains of transactions require each vendor and buyer and their solicitors to be as effective and efficient as it is possible to be if each set of contracts is to be exchanged on the same day with all the documentation properly completed. Regular communication and dealing with paperwork promptly, therefore, can help avert disaster.

Specific problems include:

The building society or bank will not lend you the full amount as a consequence of the surveyor's valuation

You must ask yourself if the lender is justified in refusing to lend the full amount. Is the property worth less than your offer figure in view of the work that needs doing to it?

Whatever the reason for the lender's withholding the full amount that they had agreed, in principle, to lend you on the basis of your salary, you have four options:

a) you can attempt to renegotiate the price with the vendor

b) you can negotiate with the lender that you undertake to have the necessary work done and that they undertake to make stage payments

c) you can reduce your contingency budget (refer to the additional costs checklist in Chapter 1)

d) you can arrange private finance through a friend or relative.

In the case of options (c) and (d), you should appreciate that you are, in fact, paying the full offer price, despite the fact that the lender's valuer is of the opinion that the property is not worth it.

Your own survey is awful in a number of respects and you have serious doubts about proceeding

a) You should renegotiate the price *or*

b) you should withdraw and look for a better property.

Your survey mentions specific defects which you know your vendor has had treated, for example, dry rot, wet rot, woodworm infestation

Your solicitor should obtain for you the relevant guarantees in respect of work the vendor has had done, together with a written assignment of the guarantee to you as the buyer. Your solicitor should check the validity of any guarantee, that the vendor is entitled to assign it, that the company offering the guarantee is still in business and is prepared to honour the guarantee and that time is on your side – if the guarantee runs out in a month or so, there might not be time for you to make use of it.

You decide that you don't like the property any more

You should withdraw without delay. Instruct your solicitor to inform the vendor's solicitor and, as a courtesy, explain to the vendor and his estate agent that you are doing so. You may need the estate agent's goodwill if you intend to continue the search.

You are gazumped or the vendor decides either not to sell or to sell to a friend

There is nothing you can do to recover the property or the time you have wasted. Your solicitor may be able to recover from the vendor a sum in respect of your legal and surveying fees, but this is not very likely.

Your solicitor tells you that the search is holding everything up

Instruct him to have a private search done and ensure that the report is faxed or delivered by courier.

Your solicitor advises you that you are in a contract race, in which the vendor has accepted offers from two separate buyers and will sell to the first who is ready to exchange contracts

Unless your solicitor knows for a certain fact that you are well ahead of the other buyer, don't get involved unless you are prepared to risk incurring legal and surveying charges and ending up with no property.

Your solicitor advises you that the lease on the property is for less than 65 years

Unless the price reflects this, don't buy. If you do, remember that the property may be difficult to sell once the lease is shorter than 55 years, and you might lose money.

In addition, most banks and building societies are reluctant to lend on leasehold properties where the lease is relatively short. Some lenders, for example, make it a condition of a loan on leasehold properties that the mortgage is paid off with 40 years of the lease still in force. If you are seeking a 25 year mortgage, therefore, you would not be able to buy any property on a lease shorter than 65 years.

The pre-contract enquiries were completed ages ago, the contracts are ready to exchange, but your building society or bank has failed to notify your solicitor of the formal offer, although you have been told verbally that everything is going ahead.

Ask the lender to fax a copy of the formal offer direct to your solicitors, or ask the lender to mail it by special delivery or despatch it by courier, depending on the time factor.

The contracts are ready, the formal offer has been received, but the endowment policy, part of an endowment mortgage, has not yet been issued by the insurance company. Alternatively, the mortgage protection policy for use with a capital repayment policy has not surfaced.

Ask your lender for the name of the person to contact at the insurance company and the telephone number, and chase him or her up. Alternatively, ask your solicitor to do this.

Your solicitor advises you that there is a hold-up in another part of the chain, although your own documentation is all in place and exchange of contracts can take place once the rest of the chain has caught up.

Ask your solicitor to telephone the other solicitors involved in the chain to establish the cause and nature of the delay. Ask him to relay the information to any vendors and buyers who may be threatening to pull out: get him, in other words, to buy time. You could also tell your solicitor, if you want to make sure of buying your property, that you are prepared to incur extra charges in the form of faxes and couriers if necessary.

You lose the property you wish to buy, but you have a firmly committed buyer for your existing property and things are now at an advanced stage

You have several options:

a) tell your buyer of the problem and explain that you will try to find an alternative property as quickly as possible;
b) don't tell your buyer and ask your solicitor to engage in delaying tactics while you search for an alternative property;
c) prepare yourself for a double move, first into rented property and later into a property that you have been able to find at your leisure (if house prices are rising sharply, however, you may lose money by doing this);

d) call off your sale and start the process of buying and selling all over again.

You lose your buyer, but you would hate to lose the property that you are about to purchase.

You have two options:

a) Find another buyer as quickly as possible and at the same time tell your solicitor to delay as far as is possible on your purchase. Take your solicitor's advice about whether or not you should advise the vendor of this potential problem. If your vendor is anxious to sell, and it happens to be a seller's market, it may be better to keep quiet until you have found a second buyer.

b) Go ahead with your purchase, appreciating that you may have to apply to your bank for a bridging loan. This is a very expensive form of finance and should be avoided if at all possible.

If you are faced with this difficult dilemma and you decide to try for another buyer, do everything you can to sell as quickly as possible:

- instruct at least three estate agents
- make sure that the property is advertised in the national Sunday newspapers
- make sure that the agents have your daytime and evening telephone numbers.
- agree to show the property at short notice and at whatever time of day the prospective purchasers wish to view
- keep the property unbelievably clean and tidy; clean the windows, get rid of old newspapers and clean out the ashtrays
- when prospective purchasers come to view, make sure there is nothing to distract them: turn off the television, tether the dogs, and bribe the children to keep quiet
- don't let the purchaser know that you feel a bit desperate! (this is meant to be a slick operation)
- be realistic about any defects and explain that this is why the property has been priced at a bit less than it is worth. This should save time later when your prospective buyer receives the valuation and full survey.

'I'd like to measure up'

This small sample of potential disasters demonstrates just why it is essential not to set your heart on buying a particular property – in England or Wales, at any rate. It also shows that a lot of detailed forward planning may turn out to be a waste of time. There is no point, for example, in measuring up for curtains or carpets until contracts are exchanged. This has the effect of making you more psychologically and emotionally involved with the place you wish to buy, and, accordingly, will heighten your disappointment if you later have no option but to let it go.

Once you have exchanged contracts, however, with the vendor for the purchase of your new home, and with your buyer if you are also selling, you can then start the detailed planning. When the signed contracts are exchanged, you, your vendor and your buyer are all *legally bound* to go ahead with the sale.

The sale takes place formally on the day of completion, which is typically some three to four weeks after exchange of contracts, although it can, by prior arrangement, take place less than a week after you exchange, provided that the paperwork has been completed. If the purchaser pulls out after the exchange of contracts he or she will forfeit the deposit, usually 10 per cent of the purchase price, which will have been paid at the time of exchange of contracts. This would be £5000 on a £50,000 property, £10,000 on a £100,000 property and so on – a sum to reckon with. It is worth stressing that the sale takes place *formally* on the day of completion *but* each party is legally bound to go ahead *once contracts are exchanged*.

The detailed planning that you should start thinking about, directly after contracts have been exchanged, in preparation for the move into your new home is the subject of the next chapter.

5

Nearly there

Once you have exchanged contracts, you can breath a sigh of relief. There are now unlikely to be any problems affecting your purchase of your new home. Exchange of contracts poses the most important milestone in the process of buying or selling a home, not so much for what you are required to do at that time but for the implications. In essence, all that will have happened is that your solicitor will have presented you with a contract to sign for the purchase of your new home and, if you are also selling, a contract to sign for that sale. By the time of the day of exchange each vendor and each buyer will have signed their contracts, allowing each solicitor to carry out the exchange so that you have, in effect, bought your new home and sold your existing one.

After contracts have been exchanged, there normally follows a short period in which the loose ends concerning finance and property deeds are tidied up or 'completed'. Completion day, which can be a few days after exchange but is usually three or four weeks later, is the day on which you must vacate your existing home and the day on which you can move into your new home. It is most unlikely that anything will go wrong between exchange and completion; although it has been known, it is a rare event. If you are buying in Scotland, and you have had your written offer accepted, you are in the same position as if you had exchanged contracts in England and Wales.

During the period between exchange of contracts and completion the building society or bank sends a cheque for the amount of the loan to your solicitor. He will send the money needed to your vendor's solicitor, who, in return, will send the deeds of your new home to your solicitor. Your solicitor will register the title and send the deeds to the lender, who keeps them as security against the loan. You should collect the keys from the vendor's estate agent or, if there is none, the vendor on completion day.

It should be noted that the completion money is not sent to the vendor's solicitor before completion day. This step frequently takes place on the actual day of completion. If long chains are involved, this practice can result in some nerve-wracking moments for buyers in England and Wales and may involve you in telephone calls to your solicitor on the day of the move in order to check that everything is in order. Do discuss this point with your solicitor well before completion day so that last-minute hitches may be avoided.

In long chains discuss with your solicitor the question of arranging a two to three day bridging loan. This is particularly useful if you intend to move on a Friday given that neither solicitors nor financiers work at weekends. Such bridging finance would enable you to move on the day you wished to; however, you should not enter this type of arrangement unless your solicitor has a cast-iron assurance that the money is on the way.

Once contracts have been safely exchanged you can start the detailed planning for your move. You will need to think about the following in the last few weeks up to the day of the move:

1 Making an interim check on your budget.
2 Booking a removals van.
3 Arranging insurance to cover all your possessions while they are in transit on the day of the move, unless the removals company do this for you, and cover in your new home.
4 Making arrangements for the utilities such as electricity, gas, water, and telephone.
5 Paying your rates up until completion day on your existing home and arranging to pay rates on your new home from completion day.
6 Keeping in touch with your vendor, perhaps visiting your new home to measure for curtains and carpets and to be shown how things such as the central heating or cooker work.
7 Arranging with the Post Office for redirection of your mail.
8 Sending out change of address notes.

9 Making arrangements for children, elderly members of the family and pets on the day of the move.

10 Returning rented equipment, such as a television or video, or arranging with the hire company that it may be moved to your new address.

11 Liaising with any contractors for work you already know will have to be carried out shortly after you have moved in.

12 Home security – do you intend to change or add to the locks, or do you intend to have a burglar alarm installed, for example?

13 Arranging for final deliveries and final bills from those who call regularly, such as the milkman or newsagent.

14 Working out a detailed plan of your new home and deciding, in principle, at least, into which room each of your possessions is destined to go. This can save both you and the removals firm (see Chapter 6) a great deal of time and energy. It also helps you to identify what you need and what you don't need

15 A couple of days before completion day, label everything you possess in order that the removals men put it in the correct room in your new home. You may wish to pack for yourself anything that is valuable, personal or delicate.

16 Keep back a large suitcase and a large cardboard box, into which you can pack essential supplies (see Chapter 6) for the day of the move and the first few days in your new home.

17 Reassess your budget, taking into account any expenses you have incurred since exchange of contracts by referring to points 2–13 above. What you have left from your overall budget may be put towards a contingency fund for the unforeseen expenses that are almost bound to arise after you have moved and for carpets or other floor coverings, kitchen equipment, furniture and curtains.

Let's now look at some of these points in more detail.

An interim budget

Most of us go over budget when we move house, so it is a good idea to check the budget now and again to prevent it becoming completely out of control. Once you have exchanged contracts with the vendor, you will have more precise information about the legal, surveying, financial and estate agency costs, outlined in the fixed costs checklist on pages 7–11 of Chapter 1. You will also know what your monthly mortgage repayments and rates payments are to be. You should then consider any additional costs, as outlined in the checklist on page 22 of Chapter 1. What you have left is, I am afraid, going to be eaten into somewhat by the things described in this chapter, so take a look now at the checklist above (points 2–13). You should also bear in mind that there will almost certainly be completely unforeseen expenses after you have moved in.

Removals

If you are a first-time buyer at present living in furnished accommodation, it may be that you can move all your possessions in a hired van with friends to help you. Once you are established with large items of furniture, such as a double bed and a sofa, for example, you will probably need a firm of professional removers. You should obtain three quotations from such firms, choosing them according to a friend's personal recommendation, from those registered with the British Association of Removers or from the *Yellow Pages* directory.

Give them the date of the move, the details of your new home (including any potential difficulties such as a basement entrance or narrow stairs) and any special instructions for fragile objects. They will furnish you with quotes and probably offer to effect insurance cover for your possessions for the day of the move. Although you may already have a householder's comprehensive policy, most of your possessions will be covered only if they are *in* your home.

Once you accept one firm's quotation, they will probably

expect you to pay in advance for their work. If you don't wish to, offer them 10 per cent on agreement and the remainder on completion of the work. They may or may not agree.

Insurance cover

You should advise your insurers that you intend to move and the date of the move, so that they may amend their records. You need to make sure that your possessions are covered up to and including completion day at your existing home, while they are in transit and at your new home from, and including, the day of completion. (Transit cover may be arranged by the removers.)

Services

You should notify your local electricity board, gas board, water board and British Telecom of the date on which you intend to move and arrange for final bills to be sent to you. You should check with your purchaser that he or she wishes all these utilities to remain connected and instruct the relevant organizations accordingly.

You should also contact the local electricity board, gas board, water board and British Telecom in respect of your new home, advising them of the date you are moving in, that you wish to take over the service, and that you do not wish it to be disconnected. Your vendor should have arranged with them to receive final bills, but you can double-check this if you wish.

The general rates and water rates

The general rates are often sorted out by the solicitor, but not always. It is up to you to make sure that the relevant council is advised of the date on which you intend to take over the property (completion day). Rates should have been paid by the vendor up until that date.

Keeping in touch

It often proves worthwhile to keep in touch with your vendor in the period between exchange and completion. You will be able to ask about all sorts of things in the much more relaxed atmosphere that normally prevails after exchange. You may want to measure up for curtains and so on and find out how the boiler works so that you have water and heat soon after you move in. Ask your vendor where the main stopcock and the fuse box are, too. You could also ask if they intend to leave the lightbulbs – many people do not!

You will also have the opportunity, most important if you are moving to a new area, to ask the vendor about the local doctor, dentist, vet, post office, library, drycleaners, milk delivery, newsagent, window cleaner, plumber, electrician, general builder and anything else you would like to know.

Getting your mail forwarded

Three options present themselves: you can keep returning to your old home to collect it; you can ask your buyer to forward it; or you can pay the Post Office for a period of up to a year to forward it automatically so that, instead of being delivered to your old address, any mail, irrespective of how it is addressed, will be delivered to your new home. If you decide to do this, you can obtain a Redirection of Mail form from any branch of the Post Office.

Change of address

A note of your new address and telephone number, and the date from which they will apply, should be sent to all your family and friends, work colleagues who need to know plus:

- your bank
- your insurers
- credit card companies, including store cards

- Driver Vehicle Licensing Centre, Swansea SA6 7JL, with details of your car and registration (failure to do so risks a £400 fine)
- your motor insurers
- DoH and DSS
- your doctor
- your dentist
- hospital, if you are currently receiving treatment
- anyone with whom you have a hire purchase agreement
- mail order companies
- tax office
- pensions, through the Post Office
- children's schools
- professional advisers, including accountant and stockbroker
- anyone to whom you pay a standing order from your bank
- subscriptions for club memberships, magazines etc.
- television licence, through the Post Office
- professional associations
- Premium Bond Office
- your children's friends
- childminders
- children's activities, such as playgroups, Brownies, Cubs and any clubs

A smooth move

If you have children, elderly live-in relatives or pets, you would be well advised to make special arrangements in advance for them on the day before the move and the day itself. Try to get someone to look after the children or, if this is impossible, make sure that you give them either something useful to do or something that will keep them amused so that you can get on with all the last-minute jobs in peace.

As for pets, all except dogs will need some sort of container in which to travel to your new home, so make sure you have what you need well before you are due to move. Pets such as cats and dogs usually sense that something is up and may disappear just when you need them. It is probably best to shut any cats in an empty room with food, water and a cat tray until you are ready to put them in their cat baskets. Make sure that the room is secured so that no one lets them escape. Cats are almost certain to disappear, unless they are contained, but dogs are not so predictable: they may just stick around and look mournful and keep tripping people up. You may find it easier to put them into kennels the day before the move and collect them a day or two after you have moved. If, on the other hand, your garden is secure, they might be happier there while the removal is going on.

Where is it to go?

The next thing to do is to make a detailed room-by-room plan of your new home and to mark on it where you would like each piece of furniture to be. The plan should include the cooker, fridge, any other large objects destined for the kitchen (such as a washing machine), sofa, armchairs, bookcases, tables, piano, hi-fi, television, video, dining table and chairs, desks, beds, chests of drawers, wardrobes, cupboards, bedside tables and anything else which it would be helpful to you not to have to move again after the removers have all left.

The plan has three purposes: first, to make the move itself as easy and quick as possible (see Chapter 6); secondly, to make sure that your possessions will fit in (it would be a good idea to sell anything that doesn't *before* you move); and, thirdly, to identify anything that you will need but don't possess. First-time buyers, for example, may have to start from scratch, buying essentials such as a cooker and a bed. You'll need to think about all these things well before you move.

If you find you have things to sell, offer them to friends, advertise them in the local paper, offer them to second-hand shops or auction houses or, if they are valuable, to specialist dealers. Don't waste time and money on moving anything that you don't like or anything that won't fit in.

Another look at the budget

Take another look, now, at your budget, shortly before you are to move and see how things are working out. There are bound to be things you would like to buy for your new home, but it is essential, if you are to avoid a tidal wave of debt, to make sure you have kept back enough to meet essential expenses.

These essential expenses comprise:

- those listed from 1 to 13 at the start of Chapter 1
- some of those listed from 1 to 10 toward the end of Chapter 1
- some of those from 2 to 13 at the start of this chapter
- the unpredictable, unforeseen expenses that are almost certain to surface within the first three months in your new home, as most people do not bother to carry out repairs once they know they are going to move

With these thoughts in mind, it is best to delay buying non-essential items such as curtains, for example. If, on the other hand, there are things you cannot do without, you may as well buy them now while you have the time. Although there are a lot of things to do before you move, you will be much busier after you move.

Doing things cheaply

It's worth looking around for bargains and doing things as cheaply as possible, even if you don't have to. It's nice to know that you will be able to afford to go on holiday at some time in the future, after all. It's well worth looking around for those things that you know you'll have to buy in the few quiet weeks between exchange and completion, while you are still living in a reasonably ordered home. Once you have moved, your time will be taken up with unpacking. If you buy anything which has to be delivered, see if you can arrange to have it delivered after your move to your new address.

Good sources of bargains include local newspapers, newsagents' postcards, second-hand shops, auction houses, furniture emporia, car boot sales and magazines such as *Exchange & Mart*.

If you are looking for desks, either for children or adults, make for second-hand office equipment shops listed under 'Office Equipment' and under 'Second-hand Dealers' in the *Yellow Pages* directory.

Let's look at floorcoverings first. The cheapest option for a long-lasting kitchen floor is vinyl. After that in ascending order of cost are carpet tiles, lino, cork tiles and quarry tiles. If there already exists some form of kitchen floor covering, it is almost certainly better not to renew it until you have been in your new home for a month or so, so that the old covering takes the initial heavy wear. If there is no covering at all, as there often isn't in new flat conversions, large rush mats or fitted coconut matting from any branch of Habitat will provide you with a reasonable covering at not too great an expense. Neither will last as long as vinyl, however, nor so easy to clean.

The other rooms of your new home can be carpeted with second-hand carpet, carpet from a wholesale warehouse or with coconut matting. Coconut matting is not really suitable for a bathroom, so go for carpet or cork tiles here. You can buy tiles from DIY shops and lay them yourself, provided that the bathroom is well ventilated (the fumes from the adhesive are potentially toxic).

Most kitchen equipment, machines, and crockery can be obtained second-hand, or at cut prices during the January and July sales. It is probably wiser, however, to buy things like fridges and washing machines new in a sale rather than second-hand, unless you are buying from a trusted friend. Gas cookers are less temperamental and therefore a safer bet to buy second-hand. The January and July sales are a good source of reduced china and sometimes cutlery as well.

Most furniture can eventually be found second-hand. The trick here is to avoid buying something that you can see will need to be professionally reupholstered and covered. This is very expensive work and you would find it cheaper to buy new from one of the stores offering interest-free credit, ideally during one of the sales. Alternatively, you could put off buying upholstered furniture such as sofas and armchairs and use cushions instead.

These are cheap and easy to make yourself, obtaining bags of foam pieces from street markets or specialist suppliers, calico for the inside cover, again from a street market, and the outside covering either from street markets or from stores during their January or July sales, when slightly imperfect fabrics are sold at comparatively low prices.

Upright dining chairs can be found in second-hand shops and, if you buy several unmatched single chairs rather than a set, you will save quite a bit of money. Dining tables, again, can be found in second-hand shops or at auctions.

A bed is an almost unavoidable expense, unless you are prepared to use a futon, sunbed, Z-bed, camp bed or lilo. Decent second-hand beds can be obtained through local newspaper ads or through a good-quality second-hand dealer.

Curtaining an entire house can prove a formidable expense, but there are ways round this. Fabrics such as muslin or calico can be used to provide soft, falling drapes, rather than the structured look of traditional curtains. Alternatively, if you go to auctions regularly, you are bound to come across good-quality velvet, brocade or damask curtains sooner or later – check measurements before you buy. You will also quite often see second-hand curtains advertised in your local newspaper. Blinds are a cheaper alternative to curtains, but they are not in fact cheap unless you buy stock sizes or you make them yourself. You can buy blind-making kits, complete with roller, fixings and stiffening spray for the fabric. Blinds, too, can be picked up second-hand.

It is clearly not a good idea to try to buy absolutely everything you may need for your new home before you move, but it is well worth using the quiet time before you move, once you are certain that your purchase is definite, to look for things such as reasonably priced carpeting and furniture. Do be certain in your mind before you buy that each item is the right colour, size or shape. Most of us revise our ideas once we've moved – and have new ideas! – about what we need and about suitable colours. So, look around by all means, but remember that furnishing your new home may span several months, from a few weeks before you move to three or four months or more after you've moved.

Lastly, if you are looking for gardening equipment and tools, it's best to leave it until the late autumn when the demand is at its lowest. The best source is local newspaper advertisements and newsagents' cards.

Moving at last

The day of your move is approaching quickly, so now is the time to run through the checklist of the things you need to do, using the checklist on pages 82–3 as a guide. There are just two more things to turn your attention to in the last week or so before The Move. First, ring your solicitor to check that completion is set for the date arranged and ask him whether you have to vacate your home at a particular time and at what time your new home will be ready to move into. Keys are sometimes left with the estate agent for the new owner to collect, but check this with your solicitor or the vendor's agent.

The second task is to think about cleaning and drycleaning about a week before the day of the move. There is nothing worse than moving into a new home with dirty, dusty or greasy possessions! You'll probably be much too busy unpacking, in any case, once you've moved to have time for this sort of cleaning. If you are taking your own curtains, for example, it makes sense to have them cleaned before you move, and leave them in polythene for the move, and you can then hang them without delay after you move.

Packing, the last few days in your old home and the move itself are the subject of the next chapter.

6

The day of the move

In the last few days before the move itself, you will probably be preoccupied with all sorts of details, and tidying up loose ends from the matters you attended to in the weeks after exchange of contracts, as described in the previous chapter. You may find it helpful to keep a notebook and jot down 'jobs for the day'. Do double-check that you have seen to the checklist on pages 82–3.

In the last two or three days before the move itself, you will probably be dealing mostly with:

1 Your detailed room-by-room plan, described in Chapter 5, which you can refer to when you come to labelling your large possessions.
2 Labelling every single thing that is not to be packed into a carton, such as furniture and kitchen appliances.
3 If you are using professional removers, deciding on which items you would prefer to pack yourself.
4 Packing a suitcase for each member of the family with the things they will need for a week.
5 Packing a box of essential last-minute items, such as tea-making equipment, food, soap, loo paper and things that you may need as soon as you are into your new home.
6 A telephone call to your solicitor to check that everything is set for 'completion', the day of your move.
7 Arranging where to leave the keys of your present home and from where to collect the keys for your new home.
8 Covering any furniture that may mark or stain during the move, such as sofas and upholstered chairs, with polythene sheeting or bed sheets.
9 Final bills – have the bills for electricity, gas, telephone, milk and newspapers all come in and been paid?
10 Planning a simple supper, or a meal out, the night before the move when a lot of your things may already be packed.

Room-by-room plan

This is invaluable, as we saw in Chapter 5, for three reasons: you can decide where each of your possessions is to be placed in your new home; you can give a copy of the plan to the removers, so that, once you are in, you don't have to waste time and energy moving everything around again; and you can identify those things that you don't like, don't work, or won't fit in. There's no point in moving any of these! Keep the plan handy, particularly on the day of the move. You will find it especially useful if you have many pieces of furniture.

Labelling your possessions

This makes the job quicker for the removers, as they then don't need to keep consulting the room-by-room plan. You should also label any anonymous cardboard boxes with the contents, so that you don't have to rifle through a dozen boxes for one particular item after you move into your new home.

While you are doing this, don't overlook the items that you have agreed to sell to your buyer. You'll have listed these at an earlier stage and given a copy of the list to your solicitor. Use it now to help you identify all the things that are not to be packed and removed. Mark these 'Do not remove – these stay here' so that they do not inadvertently find themselves in the removals van.

Packing special items

If you are using professional removers, they will pack and move absolutely everything for you, unless you give them special instructions to the contrary. You may, for example, want to pack your own jewellery, passport, correspondence, underwear and toiletries. It is best to pack these things before the removers arrive and keep them separate from the things you wish the removers to pack.

Experienced professional removers can pack fragile items, such as porcelain or antique clocks, better and faster than most of us. If you have any doubts about how careful removers are likely to be, pack such items yourself in lots and lots of newspaper and place them in a sturdy cardboard box. Secure and label the box and mark it 'FRAGILE'. The same applies to hi-fi equipment and videos.

If you do pack some items yourself, you should check if this affects your insurance cover. If the removers have effected insurance for you, it may be a condition of cover that items are covered only if packed by the removers. Items such as jewellery, however, would be covered, provided that you have All Risks cover under a Householder's Comprehensive policy, whether they are moved in the removals van or by you.

What will we need?

If you are moving a family with a lot of possessions, you will find it helpful after you have moved in if you have packed a suitcase for each member, containing everything you think they will need for a week or so. Otherwise, as soon as someone wants something, they'll have to explore the contents of a dozen boxes or more before they find it.

Children's suitcases should contain clothes, shoes, paper and pens, lots of toys and things that will keep them happy while you unpack, washing things, shampoo, and a towel. Adults will need clothes, including old clothes for unpacking and emergency DIY, plus anything you may need in a hurry – such as your address book – and things that you normally use every day.

Essential items

In The Box go tea bags, coffee-making equipment, coffee, milk, sugar, kettle (plus lead); mugs; biscuits; food for supper on the day of the move and for breakfast the following morning; pet food; soap and hand towel; loo paper; light bulbs; aspirin and Elastoplast; disinfectant, such as Dettol; washing-up liquid; teacloth; paper and pen (as the telephone is bound to ring just as you are moving in); scissors and string; Copydex and sellotape;

three sizes of screwdriver; and a hammer. This Box represents your lifeline to sanity when all around you is chaos.

Packing and removal

You have packed your personal things and The Box, made arrangements for the children, and any elderly live-in relatives and pets, and now await your removers. Greet them with tea and biscuits and a warm smile, and hope for the best.

You will probably need to talk to them about some of the following:

- anything that you may be leaving in your home, and should therefore not be packed and removed
- anything that you have already packed and intend to transport yourself and should therefore not be put in the removals van
- identifying the contents of each carton as it is packed
- the time at which you should have vacated your home and the time at which they would like to take a lunch break.

As each carton is packed, write on the outside what it contains, as this helps to reduce the feeling of complete muddle and disorientation that besets most of us when we move house.

There is no reason why anything should go wrong now, but keep your wits about you anyway. Professional removers much prefer to be left in peace to get on with their job, and find it very distracting if they are required to chat and pack at the same time. They often resent 'interference' as well, never mind that it's your possessions they are packing and it's you who are paying.

Once everything is packed up, time for one last cup of tea and a thorough check that nothing has been missed and, just as important, a check that anything your buyer has agreed to buy, such as curtains and carpets, have been left. Go through each room methodically, making sure that it is empty apart from any items that are intended to be left; open any cupboards or drawers, check fitted wardrobes and shelves. Check outside, as well, for any garden equipment. Turn off the lights, and the water and heating as well, unless your buyer is due to arrive shortly. Leave the keys at the agreed place, and off you all go.

Your new home

You've picked up the keys, you have arrived and it is yours at last. After all the doubts and difficulties that many of us encounter in buying a new home and moving into it, a sense of euphoria is hard to resist – even though at this point one is really meant to be concentrating on getting everything off the removal van into this cherished new home.

In my own most recent move, which was from London to the country, I ran round to look at the garden as soon as we arrived. I felt an overwhelming sense of bliss and relief – despite the fact that it was raining heavily, Pinbox the cat was wailing and looking morose, my husband looked bewildered by it all and it was clear that the removers were less than efficient. In fact, they left behind them a carnage of a ruined sofa, damaged desk, typewriter and filing cabinets, chipped piano, broken china and several squashed lampshades. Moving house is seldom simple, seldom without its difficulties for any of us.

If it is raining when you move, do make sure that the removers use the blankets that they normally keep in their vans to cover large items of furniture that may be damaged by water. Our sofa was ruined simply because the removals van had a leaking roof, and the rain had descended upon it. As it was a pale colour, it was badly watermarked and, eventually, had to be recovered.

When you get into the house, give the removers a copy of your room-by-room plan and show their leader each room so that they know which is which. Then offer another cup of tea. Don't, whatever you do, try and hurry them, because this will almost certainly lead to disaster – and breakages. If they appear to be working at a frenzied pace, and you can see that furniture is being damaged and chipped in front of your eyes, do whatever you can to try and slow them down. I gathered later that our removers were in a tremendous hurry because it was a Friday afternoon and they wanted to be off on time, but, unfortunately for us, were running late.

If you spot any damage or breakages while the removers are still there, point them out as politely as you can and ask their leader to sign and date a note that describes the item and the damage. This will prove invaluable when you make your insurance claim. You should ask the insurers for a claim form to be sent to you within a few days of discovering the damage.

You have moved in

The removers have gone and you are here. Surrounded by boxes, but here all the same. Don't try and do too much this first day – it's better to pace yourself a bit so that you have enough energy for the days to come. You will have to make up beds, of course, and think about food. Now's the time to take a break and look after children, any elderly live-in relatives and your pets – all of whom are probably feeling more confused and disoriented than you are. If you have a dog, this is probably a good point at which you could all take a break and go for a walk. Do remember, though, that burglars notoriously strike just as one has moved in, so check that the place is secure. If you have any doubts about the security of your home, consult without delay the Crime Prevention Officer at your local police station, a locksmith (there are plenty in the *Yellow Pages* directory) or a burglar alarm company (your local Crime Prevention Officer will supply you with a list of approved companies).

Leave the unpacking for tomorrow!

7

Your new home

The best thing about moving into your new home is that you no longer have any deadlines to keep to. The valuation, survey, mortgage application, exchange of contracts and completion are all behind you. Keeping to deadlines can be very wearying, particularly when things are beyond your own control. So, this is the time to sit back and take stock of the jobs you would like to do and the logical order in which they should be done.

Keeping a fairly detailed list of what needs to be done is the basic requirement of good forward planning. Planning is essential if you are not to waste time and energy. Planning does not prevent things going wrong, but it does prevent you from overlooking important things and helps get things done in the most logical, labour-saving way. You'll find that the process of planning is also quite a restful activity – you can't see to anything else while you are doing it and it makes you sit down for a while. Because of this, most of us are at our most creative when we sit down to plan a project, and so some of the best ideas are produced during planning.

What needs to be done first?

Make a list of what needs to be done, in any order, and then reorder all your tasks and projects so that one follows another in a logical fashion. You'll probably need to take into account some of the following, in this order:

- any building or construction work and security fixtures
- specialist treatments, for dry rot, wet rot, woodworm or other infestations
- rewiring
- replumbing
- installation or overhaul of central heating
- installation of kitchen equipment, such as cooker, washing machine, and dishwasher

- installation of telephone or additional extensions
- sweeping the chimneys (this is often necessary, even in smokeless zones, and is best done before the room is carpeted and furnished)
- redecoration
- building in cupboards, shelves and fitted wardrobes
- laying the carpets or other floorcoverings
- furnishing, and making final decisions about where all your possessions are to be
- finishing your unpacking and putting the final touches with pictures and ornaments and so on.

You can see from looking at this list that you can save yourself time, money and energy by looking at the fundamentals first. There is no point, for example, in furnishing a damp room to your satisfaction without having had the damp problem treated: the dampness in the air will gradually affect everything in the room, including books, papers, pictures and the curtain fabric itself, making it look limp; damp rooms are also expensive to heat.

The hidden snags

The two main ones are these: first, your move has probably cost more than you thought it would – this happens to practically all of us, no matter how good the financial planning is; secondly, when you move in you will almost certainly discover that there are things to be done that you had not foreseen, and these will affect your budget.

So, once you have your action plan in front of you, take another look at your budget and decide on what you can afford to do now and what you would like to put off until Year Two. It is still worth putting the fundamentals first, so rewiring, for example, should still come before carpeting and curtaining. Otherwise, when you decide that you could afford to rewire, you would have to take up the floorcoverings and store them before you could have the floorboards up.

As for being unable to foresee everything that you would

either want or need to do to your new home, this, again, happens for two reasons. The first is that the previous owner, your recent vendor, will have been reluctant to carry out repairs, essential or otherwise, once he knew he would soon be moving. As the process of selling a property and moving out typically takes three to four months and the decision to do so would probably have been made some time before that, it is often the case that no repairs will have been carried out for over six months before a buyer takes possession of his or her new home.

The second reason for unforeseen expense is, in a nutshell, enthusiasm. Most of us, when we move into a new home, are thrilled with it and want to make it look as elegant and comfortable as possible. All sorts of new ideas come to us as a result; it is only after you have moved in that you can see the possibilities for creating this and that and buying new this, new that. If you have invested in new carpeting, you might look twice at your old curtains or your old armchair . . . and this is when problems with the budget start. Restraint and a watchful eye on the budget are the only suggestions I can offer; don't forget that monthly mortgage repayments still have to be made, along with all your other regular outgoings.

Serious problems

The two categories of serious problem you may be faced with are potentially expensive defects in the property which were not noticed by your surveyor; and money, or the lack of it.

If you discover serious defects which were not mentioned in your surveyor's report but must be remedied, you can either instruct your solicitor to confront and possibly sue your surveyor for the cost of the works and for compensation for distress and inconvenience, or you can raise the money to have the work done. Those of us who have tried to sue negligent surveyors will agree that it is difficult, expensive, time-consuming and far from guaranteed to succeed. This is most unfair to the innocent consumer, but this is the reality of the situation.

It may well prove the better course of action to cut your losses and pay for the work to be done, even though this will mean delay in being able to afford such 'luxuries' as curtains and so on. A colleague of mine, the editorial director of a publishing company, bought a house in 1987 with a delightful ancient oak-beamed kitchen. Some three weeks after she, her husband and her newborn baby moved in, she found mushrooms growing in the kitchen. Dry rot was diagnosed, and the entire woodwork had to be gutted and destroyed. The kitchen was, of course, unusable, and so the spare room had to be fitted out with a microwave so that she could prepare the baby's feeds and produce food for herself and her husband.

I expressed surprise that she did not intend to sue the surveyor, but she, probably rightly, said, 'In the long run, it will be sorted out quicker by seeing the bank manager and raising the extra money.' She had had a survey and a specialist report, and so she had been satisfied that nothing was wrong. She had regarded the kitchen as one of the best features of the house, but she was compelled to replace all the cupboards and shelves with the cheapest, factory-made alternatives. My own experience now tells me that she was very probably correct in deciding that an attempt to sue a surveyor is fraught with difficulties and often unlikely to succeed.

If, on the other hand, you discover anything that you know is under guarantee, then do pursue this. If, for example, the property had been treated for dry rot or wet rot before you took it on, you should be in possession of the guarantees and you should be able to get the company who did the earlier work to return and carry out the remedial works for no charge. Do consult your solicitor if you experience any problems in resolving matters such as this.

Dealing with workmen

Some builders and specialist contractors are cheerful people who do a good job of work, on time, for the figure specified. This is the ideal. Unfortunately, a substantial number are lazy, careless, messy, noisy and carry out inferior work for a figure that increases daily from the original estimate. Moving home is taxing enough, but builders may test you to the limit of your endurance. Understanding their language will help, and remember that they won't be with you for ever:

When they say they'll be back 'first thing in the morning', this means at any time during the following day from 8 till 4.

'Thirsty work this' declared as they enter means they want a cup of tea, now, with lots of sugar.

'Terrible, isn't it?' means they want to discuss with you what they've just read in the *Sun*.

'Time for lunch soon' saves you having to look at your watch – it'll be shortly after 11 a.m.

'The afternoon always drags, doesn't it?' means more tea and biscuits, too, if they think you'll run to it.

'Can't be done' means *they* are not going to do it. 'Could be done' means only if you pay more money. 'You could do that yourself' means they're off home and you'd better have done it by 'the following morning' so as not to hold them up.

'There, that's straight now' means either that the speaker is blind or else he's offering you a challenge.

'That'll be dry by tomorrow' meaning that the paint will be too tacky to allow the carpet fitters in to do their work.

'Wonder where that's coming from' means they've drilled through a water pipe. 'Gets dark quickly these days, doesn't it' means they've drilled through an electric cable and fused everything in your home.

'Oh, that won't take long to shift' alerts you to the fact it will take you two days to clear up all their rubbish and take it to the local tip.

What can be done? I have no answers: I can only suggest that you follow these golden rules.

1 Specify the work to be done in writing.
2 Let them proceed only after you have agreed to a firm quotation (not an estimate).
3 Refuse to make interim payments with the words 'Oh, I don't think it's worth the bother, you'll be finished soon'.
4 Check personally every stage and every aspect of the work.

5 Make them redo anything that's badly or wrongly done.
6 Pay them only after the work has been satisfactorily completed and after you have received your guarantee (if applicable), making sure you get a signed and dated receipt for the work before they disappear.

Your verdict

You will probably be quite well settled in, with all the teething problems sorted out, within three months or so of your move. This is the time to sit back and decide whether it has all been worth it. I hope that you will feel it has, as many of us do. If, on the other hand, you have serious doubts, do remember that buying a new home and moving into it is a very stressful and disorienting process, which will have preoccupied you for several months and that this can take its toll, even on the most cheerful of us. Given a little longer, you may feel better about it all, and more on top of the large financial investment you have made.

Most of us say that moving home is an experience not to be repeated quickly, but of the 62 per cent of us who own our own homes, many of us move again . . . and again. Moving is such an expensive activity, however, that you would be wise to allow two years, at least, to elapse before moving again. If, for example, your moving costs came to £6000 and you stay in that property for two years, it will have cost you £3000 each year. If, however, you stay in your home for six years, the move would have cost you £1000 each year. If you move frequently, you are, in effect, reducing your assets by spending money on something that you could avoid. The best way of avoiding this is, of course, making the right decision when you do move: when you're house-hunting, look at a number of properties, don't do it in a hurry, make sure that you buy at a reasonable price, and plan the entire process as carefully as you can so that you can feel confident of coping successfully with moving house.

Index